The Pure Life

The Heart of the Matter

The Pure Life

The Heart of the Matter

by Lori Wagner
and Gwyn Oakes

The Pure Life
The Heart of the Matter

by Lori Wagner and Gwyn Oakes

© 2014 Ladies Ministries, UPCI
2nd printing 2019

Cover and Interior Design: Laura Merchant

Bible translations used: Unless otherwise noted, the King James Version is the primary Bible translation used. Also included for reference are the New King James Version, New International Version, New American Standard Bible, Common English Version, and Amplified Bible.

All rights reserved. No portion of this publication may be reproduced, stored in an electronic system, or transmitted in any form or by any means, electronic, mechanical, photocopy, recording, or otherwise, without the prior permission of the author(s). Brief quotations may be used in literary reviews.

Printed in United States of America

More to Life
THROUGH GOD'S WORD

A *More to Life* Publication
36 Research Park Court
Weldon Spring, MO 63304

Table of Contents

Acknowledgments 7
Foreword 9
Introductory Story 11
Chapter One: Purity 101 15
Chapter Two: All of Me for All of Him 27
Chapter Three: Looking Back and Moving Forward 37
Chapter Four: Heart Start 45
Chapter Five: Pure Vision 69
Chapter Six: Pure Soul 85
Chapter Seven: Pure Mind 93
Chapter Eight: Physical Purity 109
Chapter Nine: Purity Plans 133
Chapter Ten: Waiting (It's Worth It!) .153
Chapter Eleven: Restoration 163
Parting Words 179
Endnotes 185

Acknowledgments

Thank you to all who contributed to *The Pure Life*,
with special recognition to:

Sarah Hogan
Jonathan and Lindsi Walker
Stephanie and Melanie Well

"Flee also youthful lusts: but follow righteousness, faith, charity, peace, with them that call on the Lord out of a pure heart" (II Timothy 2:22).

Foreword

Now is the time for a movement of reformation and revival in the hearts and homes of women and girls around the world. It is time to go against the flow. We believe God has brought us to the kingdom for such a time as this.

For teens, that means the willingness to follow the teachings in the Word of God when it seems all the other girls your age are consumed with beauty, guys, self, sex, and just having a good time. It also means setting your affection on Christ, guarding your heart, choosing the path of purity, and becoming more like Christ when all your peers seem to be going in an opposite direction.

For young women, it means being willing to be married or single, whichever God has for you, for His glory. It means serving the Lord without distraction and being willing to keep yourself pure as a member of the family of God. It's a call to be faithful in a world of broken promises and standing strong in the good times and the bad times.

For mothers, it means allowing God to give you a vision that the generation to come might know truth and have a pure heart for the work of His kingdom. Join in teaching and prayer for the souls of your children and your grandchildren.

Welcome to the fourth book of *The Pure Path Series*. We began with *The Girl in the Dress*, followed by *Covered by Love*, and then *Unmasked*. These books deliver a message of consecration and dedication. Purity is at the core of each of the books in *The Pure Path Series*. They have to do with outward expressions of our inner relationship with God. The things we do, both private and in public, like dressing and behaving modestly, are ways that we present ourselves in public that honor God. If you have not read those books, we encourage you to get them.

On behalf of Ladies Ministries of the United Pentecostal Church International and the contributors to this series, thank you for allowing us to share with you the precious truths of God's Word. We pray you will be blessed and encouraged as you read *The Pure Life*.

> "Only as high as I reach can I grow,
> only as far as I seek can I go,
> only as deep as I look can I see,
> only as much as I dream can I be."
> ~ Karen Ravn

Introductory Story

"Jackie, what's going on with your tablet?" Katelyn stared at the screen in her hands, a puzzled look in her bright eyes.

"That's the new whole-house Internet filter doing its job." Jackie leaned over the tablet and punched in her passcode.

"When did you get that?"

"Last week," said Jackie. "It's inconvenient at times, but to tell you the truth, I really didn't like some of the things that popped up on my screen."

"I know what you mean," said Katelyn. "Did your parents get the one our pastor recommended?"

"I'm not sure," said Jackie. She drew in a deep breath and then released a sigh. "It's sad how people can get sucked into watching things they shouldn't."

Katelyn nodded. Neither girl spoke a name, but both knew the young man in their youth group who had inspired their pastor's recommendation.

"You know, I guess I don't like to think about how easy it is to take a step in the wrong direction," said Jackie. "I mean, we all have temptations to deal with, but shouldn't we be stronger? We grew up in church. It's all we've ever known."

"That's true, but we're all just people," said Katelyn. "We're all just made out of dust, you know."

Jackie shook her head and chuckled. "That's true, but we're supposed to be *holy* dust, right?"

"Holy," Katelyn turned in her chair to look at her friend. "Now that's a word that's about as easy to nail down as a piece of Jell-O. It seems to mean different things to different people."

"Holy is what God is," said Jackie, "and what we are supposed to be."

"God is lots of things."

"That's true." Jackie twisted a loose strand of hair between her fingers. "He's lots of things I'm not."

"Don't be so hard on yourself," said Katelyn. "You are one of the sweetest girls I know, and you have a real love for God."

"I do love Him, but don't you ever wonder if you love Him enough?"

"What do you mean?"

Jackie plopped down on the couch next to the computer desk and looked up at her friend. "I mean I wonder if I love Him enough to keep myself . . . well, you know . . . ."

"Um," Katelyn searched for the right word. "Pure?"

"Yeah," said Jackie. "I've never had a real boyfriend, but I wonder what it will be like when I do and what it will feel like to be kissed."

"Well, maybe you shouldn't be thinking about that right now," said Katelyn. "It's almost like looking at things on the Internet."

"What do you mean?" Jackie pulled back, confusion written on her features.

"I mean it's best not to let your mind wonder about those things right now. You know what my mom always says, 'what you feed will grow.'"

"Yeah. She does say that quite a bit," Jackie agreed. "To tell you the truth, I have a lot of questions, but I don't really want to talk to anybody about them. It's, well, it's awkward."

"You mean like 'how far is too far?'"

"Exactly." Jackie gave a firm nod. "Do you really think it's possible in today's world to stay pure until your wedding night?"

"Hey," said Katelyn, "we're supposed to be in the world, not of it. I know everywhere you look things are out of control, but that's not for us. We belong to God, remember?"

Jackie smiled. "Of course."

"The girls at school, well, so many of them seem to just hand their hearts over to any boy who looks their way, but that doesn't seem right to me. My heart isn't cheap, and neither is my body. Jesus paid a big price for me, and I'm not just going to give myself away."

"I never really thought about it like that," said Jackie. "Some girls aren't even waiting for boys to look their way. They practically shove their bodies in their faces trying to get their attention."

"I don't get it," said Katelyn. "It seems like some girls don't put a lot of value in themselves."

"True."

"Do you remember the Bible verse we learned last week in Sunday school?"

"The one about God having plans for our lives?" asked Jackie.

"Yeah," said Katelyn. "Jeremiah 29:11. I was thinking that if God has a plan for my life, that includes my love life, right?"

A broad smile broke across Jackie's face, and a twinkle lit her eyes. "Right," she said. "I guess I need to trust God with my love life, too."

"The Bible isn't outdated," said Katelyn. "I know God has our best in mind. If He says wait, there's a good reason for waiting."

"So you don't think abstinence is old-fashioned?"

"No," said Katelyn. "God wouldn't call us to it if He wouldn't help us do it."

"Aren't you the little rhyming queen today?"

"I guess so, don't you know?"

"Don't I know what?" Jackie shook her head.

"Don't you know there's a new *Pure Path* book about purity?" Katelyn spun around in the wheeled office chair. "I can't wait to read it."

Chapter One

Purity 101

Defining purity can present a real challenge. As I prayed and pondered the subject, one word came to me that seemed to sum it all up: *faithfulness*.

Purity involves faithfulness to God. Purity means faithfulness in your heart, your mind, and in your conduct. As a single person, being pure is being faithful to your future spouse even before you are married.

In simple terms, *purity* means putting God and His Word first. When we do, trusting in His purity at work in us, the Lord will help us take care of everything else.

We're going to jump into some deep subjects, and I pray you will read with an open heart. The pure path is a journey of a lifetime. No matter how old we get, each of us should continue to work towards purity.

The writer of Proverbs tells us that silver and gold are valuable resources, but godly instruction and knowledge are greater (Proverbs 8:10). Let's grab on to the greater!

| The Bible is our roadmap on the pure path. |

Psalms and Proverbs are full of helpful information. Psalm 119 is loaded with wisdom and instructions that will help us make great choices. Psalm 119:29-30 lets us know there is a "way of truth," and when we stick with it, we will not be put to shame.

Purity has been called "a godly woman's adornment." When we hear the word *purity*, we most often think about issues of sexuality, but purity involves so much more. There's a book out that says purity is "more than just saying 'no' to you-know-what." We're going to look at the "you-know-what," but we're also going to look at many aspects of purity—straight to the heart of the matter.

Where shall we start? At the beginning, of course! Long, long ago, God's people were given what the Jews call the *Shema*. It is the confession of faith. Since the time of Moses, Jewish people of all ages have recited the *Shema* every morning and every night: "Hear, O Israel: The Lord our God is one Lord: And thou shalt love the Lord thy God with all thine heart, and with all thy soul, and with all thy might" (Deuteronomy 6:4-5).

Why is this so important? The Lord wanted them to know how to live in fellowship with Him and in His blessing.

God's desire, recorded in Deuteronomy 5:29, was "that it might be well with them, and with their children for ever!" I don't know how many exclamation marks were used in the Bible, but there was one at the end of this verse. God is excited and passionate about this. He wants what is best for His beloved children—and that includes you and me.

He said it again just a few verses later (Deuteronomy 6:3). God has our best interest at heart! OK. Let's look at the *Shema* that comes in the next verse.

What does God want His people to know first and foremost? When Moses said, "Hear, O Israel," that was like saying, "Hey, you people, listen up!" What did he say after he got their attention? The most important things: Our God is one. There's one powerful, delivering, merciful, and faithful God, and guess what? He is your God! What could be better than that?

Because God is who He is, and He's done all He's done, He requested a specific response from His people. What was God looking for? The answer is in the next verse: Love Me.

Really? That's what God was looking for? Love? Yes.

It's my thought that this desire to be loved is one of the ways God made people in His image. Don't we all have that same need to be loved? I think so. I know I do.

How are we to love the Lord? With all of our heart, with all of our soul, and with all of our might (strength).

You probably know the famous verse in the New Testament, "For God so loved the world, that he gave his only begotten Son, that whosoever believeth in him should not perish, but have everlasting life" (John 3:16). God loved His people so much that He came to earth in the form of a man. He walked among His people. He taught them. He healed those who were sick—even raised some from the dead. Ultimately, He died on a cross, where He gave Himself as a sinless sacrifice to make a bridge between sinful man and a holy God. That's love. True love gives, and God truly gave the greatest gift possible: Himself.

This Bible we live by contains the Lord's words of love. It tells us that anything and everything we are asked to do hinge on God's two greatest commandments: to love God and love others. Let's look a bit more at loving God.

Loving was in the heart of God from before the beginning of time. He didn't just speak of it in the Old Testament. Jesus mentioned the *Shema* in the New Testament:

"Jesus said to him, 'You shall love the Lord your God with all your heart, with all your soul, and with all your mind'" (Matthew 22:37, NKJV).

"And thou shalt love the Lord thy God with all thy heart, and with all thy soul, and with all thy mind, and with all thy strength: this is the first commandment" (Mark 12:30).

"And he answering said, Thou shalt love the Lord thy God with all thy heart, and with all thy soul, and with all thy strength, and with all thy mind; and thy neighbor as thyself" (Luke 10:27).

God is all about love, love, love. God gave us all of Him, and He's asking for our all in return: our heart, soul, mind, and strength.

You might have noticed in the Old Testament three things were mentioned: heart, soul, and might, and in the New Testament, four: heart, soul, mind, and strength. Jesus wasn't changing things up by throwing curve balls in the New Testament. He was helping us better understand all the *Shema,* or all that our confession of faith implied.

God desires our love and devotion to the highest degree—with every part of who we are—inner and outer. When the Israelites recited the *Shema*, they understood they were willingly surrendering their lives and all they had to the Lord who loved them and gave life to them in the first place. God was asking for pure, unpolluted, and faithful love.

PURITY DEFINED

pure
adjective \ˈpyủr\
: not mixed with anything else
: clean and not harmful in any way
: having a smooth and clear sound that is not mixed with any other sounds
  a: being thus and no other: sheer, unmitigated <*pure*folly>
    (1)**:** free from what vitiates, weakens, or pollutes
    (2)**:** containing nothing that does not properly belong
  b: free from moral fault or guilt
  c: marked by chastity: continent[1]

The word pure is related to words like:

- absolute (100 percent)
- chaste/virgin (abstaining from sexual relations)
- complete (lacking nothing)
- flawless/sinless (containing nothing inappropriate or extraneous)
- purified/refined (free of dirt, defilement, or pollution)
- straight (not crooked or perverse)
- unadulterated (free from adulterants or impurities)
- unalloyed (free of foreign elements)

You may have glossed over some of those words, and I don't blame you. But take a minute to look at them again and think about how those words apply to our relationships with God and people.

Did you do it? Good! Welcome back.

I love to study. I didn't when I was young, but I do now (so there's hope for you if you don't yet). There are wonderful books to use when studying the Bible. My two favorites are *Strong's Concordance* and *Vine's Expository Dictionary*. Don't they just sound smart? These are both available online for free, which makes it so easy to look things up.

If you want to genuinely grow in spiritual maturity, it is not enough to simply be instructed by the Word of God. You may love going to church or listening to Christian radio programs. You might assume you're growing because your knowledge is increasing. However, if you don't actually grow closer to God by allowing His Word to change you from the inside out, your head will merely continue to fill with information.

In the Old Testament, after the Law of Moses was given, all the Jews knew the hygiene guidelines. They never ate without washing their hands and using clean cups, pots, and vessels. They didn't know about bacteria or viruses; they just knew what God told them. In doing what God asked, they kept themselves from many potential diseases that science has proven to be the result of poor cleanliness. This concept applies to more than just our dinner dishes, girls. Keeping God's laws can keep us healthy!

Purity is "God's safeguards on life's dangerous trails."
~ Randy Alcorn

God gave the Law to protect His people, and He connected the Law with worship. Physical purity and cleanness were both required before entering into worship. Psalm 24:3-4 reads, "Who shall ascend into the hill of the Lord? or who shall stand in his holy place? He that hath clean hands, and a pure heart; who hath not lifted up his soul unto vanity, nor sworn deceitfully."

Did you notice in these verses God connected cleanliness with worship? The person with clean hands and a pure heart, who was not proud or dishonest, was the person God blessed.

Since the beginning of time, the Lord established contrast: dark and light, clean and unclean. God makes some things so plain it's hard to find a loophole. The fact is that sin is the opposite of purity. Sin, in a simple definition, is anything that disagrees with or violates purity, for God is pure.

Pure is "top notch." Pure is the utmost. People who want the best pursue pure things because they know having "pure" means they have the top of the line. In commercials, advertisers are promoting "pure products" and "pure pleasure." From soaps to pets, pure is best. From jewelers to drug dealers, almost everyone is concerned in one way or another with purity. God cares about purity, too. He desires purity in all we think, say, and do. Why? Because impurities separate us from Him. They slow us down, like running through knee-deep mud.

When it comes to you and me, we need to understand that we are each responsible for keeping ourselves pure. "Behold what manner of love the Father has bestowed on us, that we should be called children of God! Therefore the world does not know us, because it did not know Him. Beloved, now we are children of God; and it has not yet been revealed what we shall be, but we know that when He is revealed, we shall be like Him, for we shall see Him as He is. And everyone who has this hope in Him purifies himself, just as He is pure" (I John 3:1-3, NKJV).

God knows you and I weren't born perfect. We aren't even "born again" perfect. There is a difference between being counted as righteous or innocent and being pure. God wants to partner with us in a creative working together that will change us from the old "you" into a new and continually improving "you"! "And do not be conformed to this world, but be transformed by the renewing of your mind, that you may prove what is that good and acceptable and perfect will of God" (Romans 12:2, NKJV).

"do not be conformed to this world, but be transformed."

Paul wrote in Ephesians 4:22-24 to "put off" the ways we used to live that were corrupt because of our own deceitful desires. Instead, we should be renewed in our spirits and in our minds and "put on" the new person that was created by God in true righteousness.

WHAT DOES PURITY LOOK LIKE?

Purity means loving God more than anything or anyone else. We show that love when we obey and love God wholeheartedly and devote our lives to Him. As we pursue purity, we become more and more like Jesus and grow into the person He intends for us to become.

Purity might not be the most popular message in our culture, but knowing the difference between what God says is pure and the lies promoted in our society is extremely important. God wants us to know who we are, our value, and purpose; and all three of these elements are wrapped up in purity.

We're going to look at purity from God's perspective (which should be our perspective, right? Right!). I long for you to understand who you are as a person—your value and true identity in Him. I pray as we look at our loving Father together, we will draw close to Him. That's the best way possible to keep pure. We'll also look at some ways to overcome the many obstacles we face in living a pure lifestyle in a self-centered, sex-crazed world. I hope you will be encouraged by the rewards of purity, and rise above the compromises that tempt us to walk in less than the abundant life God desires for us. Regardless of society's decaying morality that is hurled at us through the media, "health teachers," and "experts," by God's grace we can stand tall in a world that is caving in to their cravings.

"Purity is to live according to original design."
~ Josh McDowell

Think about Adam and Eve in the Garden. They walked with God in purity, and that's the way God wants to walk with you and me now. Because of Jesus' sacrifice, when He looks at you and me, God sees us as innocent—the same way He saw Adam and Eve before the Fall.

Your "love life"—right now or in the future—may be your biggest battleground. It's one of the places we so clearly see our desires fight for first place. It's in our closest relationships we see who we love the most: God, self, or the world.

Purity is about your now. Purity is about your tomorrow. Purity is about your forever.

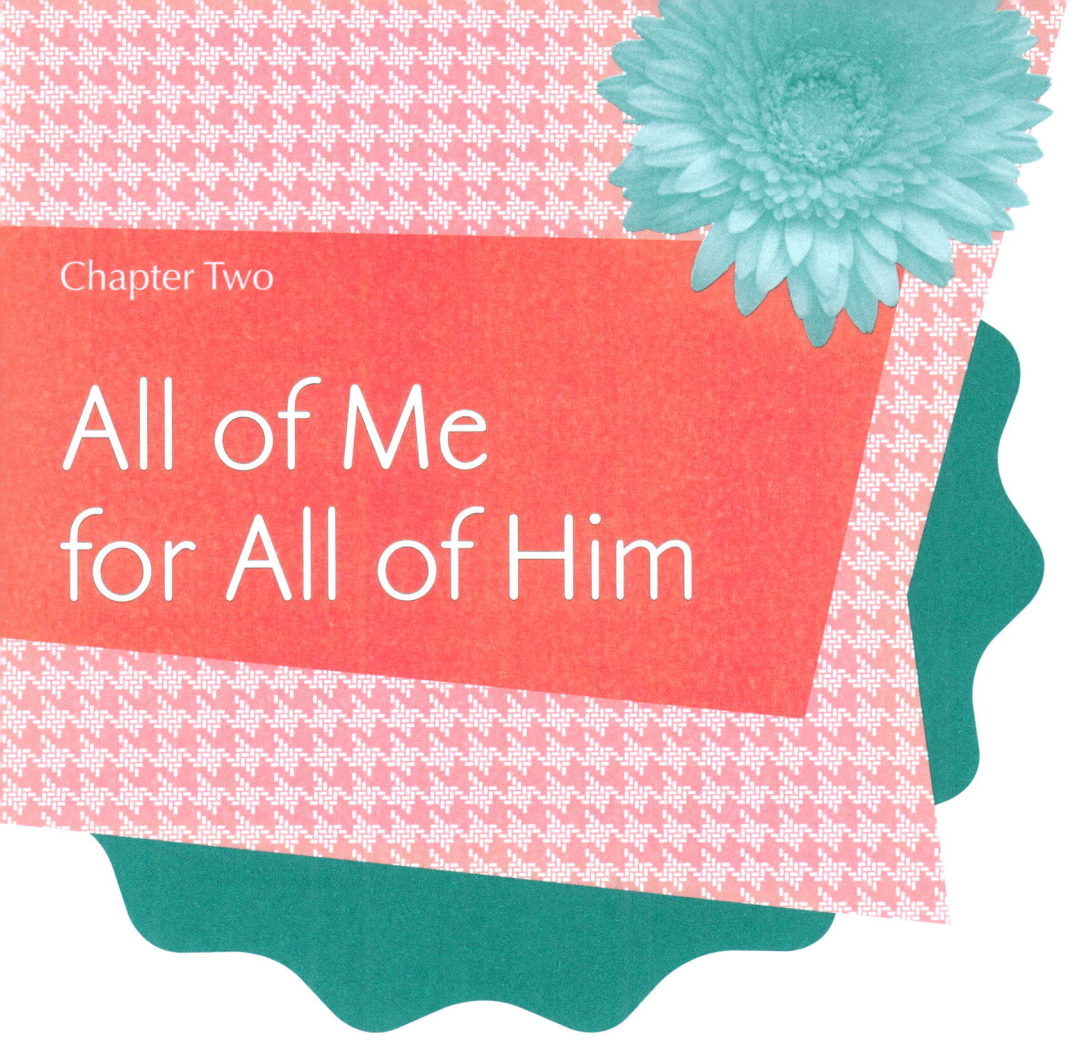

Chapter Two

All of Me for All of Him

Girls, we get the best of God's covenant. He loves us! Think about that. He knows your very worst thought. He sees you at your most unlovable moment. He knows more than you do that you could never measure up to His standards without His help. Doesn't that make you incredibly grateful for His lovingkindness and grace?

When you love someone, you want to please them. Responding to God's holiness and purity should be the natural outflow of our love for Him (I Peter 1:15-16). Scripture gives us guidelines but doesn't provide an all-inclusive list of everything we will ever face. We know some of the major do's and don'ts, but we have to know God's heart.

Reading the Bible is like getting to know the "Man" you love. If you were engaged to the coolest guy ever, you would want to know what pleases him. You would want to know his favorite food, his favorite color, what makes him barf. (Gross, I know, but what do you think an abomination is?) When we love God, we want to learn to love what He loves and get grossed out by what grosses Him out!

We may have many acquaintances, but we all have a deep need to feel truly known by those we love most.

This is because we were created in God's image—He also desires to be intimately understood and loved by us. It's not enough to know about the Lord; He wants us to learn how He thinks and feels, what's important to Him, and what His purposes are.

We can better understand God's heart and character by seeking Him and learning day by day from His Word. We come to know our friends better by sharing experiences. In the same way, we will understand God better the longer we walk with Him and meditate on what He has revealed about Himself in the Bible. God wants you to seek Him with all your heart, and He promises that when you do, you will find Him (Jeremiah 29:13). So, the next time you feel a need to be better understood, turn to the One who understands you perfectly. More importantly, ask Him to help you know Him better.

God made us to be like Him: "God created man in his own image" (Genesis 1:27). Sin changed some of our "features"—corrupting God's original design. Individually, we make the choice to continue in the sinful nature we were born with or "be conformed to the image of his Son" (Romans 8:29).

The word translated "sin" in the Old Testament comes from the Hebrew word *chatta'ath*. It means missing the mark of God's intended purpose for your life. Did you ever shoot a bow and arrow? First you load the arrow onto the bow and then pull the string

> "I think what pleases the Lord the most is when we learn from our mistakes & keep trying & growing."

back and try to line it up with the target. Once the arrow is released, it can seem like it has a mind of its own. It twists, it spins. It might hit the second field or the third, and sometimes miss the target altogether, sailing past into the wild blue yonder.

Missing the bull's-eye is a picture of *chatta'ath*, what God calls sin. Like an archer aiming for the center mark, God knows when we aim for Him and miss. That's why we can have pure hearts and still flub up from time to time. Miscalculating, misjudging, incorrect timing—all can affect the natural trajectory of an arrow and the spiritual trajectory as we shoot for God's perfect will.

God doesn't want us to feel like failures when we aren't perfect. He knows no one living in skin is without fault. What displeases Him is when we turn around and shoot at a different target, or take steps away from the goal and make it impossible to hit. I think what pleases the Lord the most is when we learn from our mistakes and keep trying and growing.

Young people as well as older face temptation every day, whether or not they are Christians. At some point most people are faced with the desire to submit to sin, whether it is gluttony, sex, gossip, cheating, or something else just as harmful to our relationship with God. Some temptations may seem minor so they are pretty easy to overcome, but other times the desire seems too great. It is important to understand that temptation is not the sin; even Jesus was tempted. We only sin when we give in to the temptation. The Bible describes *sin* as the breaking or transgression of God's law. It is also defined as disobedience or rebellion against God.

Many sins are spelled out clearly in the Bible. For example, the Ten Commandments give us a clear picture of God's laws. They offer basic rules of behavior for spiritual and moral living. Many other verses give examples of sin, but how can we know if something is sin when the Bible is not clear? God speaks to us through not only His Word but many times through our conscience. So, when there is a feeling that something is not right, it pays to follow that feeling.

Everyone is different, so it is important to know what temptations are hardest for you to overcome. For instance, some may find that gossip is more tempting than sex. Others may find that even holding a date's hand is too much of a temptation. When you know what tempts you the most, you can be prepared to avoid that temptation.

Let's look at some things that can throw our arrows off course. A good place to start is with the Ten Commandments.

What is the very first commandment? "Thou shalt have no other gods before me" (Exodus 20:3).

Now let's look at before the beginning of time. What did Satan do to get kicked out of Heaven? Isaiah 14:12-14 gives us the answer: he wanted to be like God, he wanted to be noticed, and he wanted glory.

We've all been faced with the temptation to put ourselves first—our interests, our desires. That, my friend, is a step on a path that leads to destruction. Harsh? Maybe. True? Yep.

As long as we live we will be challenged in three main areas (I John 2:16): the lust of the flesh (what our flesh wants), the lust of the eyes (what we see and then want), and the pride of life (pride in possessions). The Bible tells us that all our temptations come under one of those categories! Check it out in I John 2:16-17: "For all that is in the world, the lust of the flesh, and the lust of the eyes, and the pride of life, is not of the Father, but is of the world. And the world passeth away, and the lust thereof: but he that doeth the will of God abideth for ever."

Being holy or pure means more than just wanting to be holy or pure. Having good intentions or making pledges and vows are not enough. We have to follow Jesus' example. He was disciplined. While reading the Gospels, it might seem He wandered from place to place. He was spontaneous and responsive to people—teaching, healing, and delivering—but He had a single-minded drive: to do the will of the Father.

From His first words in Luke 2:49 to His last in Luke 23:46, Jesus always moved under the direction of His Father (John 5:19-20). The example He gave us was this: Don't do anything by yourself, in your flesh. Jesus listened to the Father and then obeyed with courage and tenacity, sealed by love.

PERFECTLY NORMAL

We desire friendship with both male and female companions. As you develop relationships in your life, remember that Jesus wants to be your most intimate friend. You can tell Him anything. He will never be shocked or disappointed. He already knows you. He knows your heart.

The best defense against impurity is to play offense. Get and stay close to God.

"Draw nigh to God, and he will draw nigh to you. Cleanse your hands, ye sinners; and purify your hearts, ye double minded" (James 4:8). Clean hands and pure hearts are linked together. Our actions, thoughts, and motives are like plates of spaghetti where one noodle is tangled up with the next. In the

same way, a person's morality is connected with every area of life. Purity involves more than sexual conduct. It includes principles like honesty, kindness, and giving.

No person is perfect. Each of us is a work in process, and although we are flawed, we are "complete in him" (Colossians 2:10). If you have a hole in your heart that you feel can't be filled until you find Prince Charming, remember that the only "him" who will ever complete you is Jesus. A relationship with another person will never make a whole, healthy person out of someone who is not whole and healthy on her own.

Knowing your destiny with God should be that catalyst that purifies your life in the here and now (I John 3:3). Living in hope, knowing you will eventually be like Jesus, should make us want to be more like Him right now. The anticipation of all the wonders to come can actually have a cleansing effect on our lives. That anticipation makes us want to please the Lord now and be ready when He comes for us, His bride.

When you and I toddled about in diapers, we were in a different stage in our lives. Everything we did was just right for our age, even though we weren't yet potty trained. We were illiterate, but we were as we should be in that season of life.

When you mature, your natural body develops and shows outward signs you are progressing from girlhood to womanhood. I hope you will take inventory of what's happening inside as well. Are you developing spiritually? Are you maturing in your faith?

There comes a time when a young lady becomes accountable for her own choices. Think about it. Babies aren't born sinless (Psalm 51:5), but it seems the Lord considers them innocent until they reach an age of accountability.

The question we living folks need to know the answer to is this: When does a young person become accountable before God for their own decisions?

Jewish tradition sets the age of accountability around twelve or thirteen. People mature at different paces, but it seems the age of accountability coincides with puberty—the time our body tells us we are moving from girlhood to womanhood.

There comes a time when we are responsible to walk with the Lord ourselves and let go of childish, selfish thoughts and actions. I'm not saying we can't giggle and snort and have a good time. I'm all about that. But as growing girls, we need to cooperate with the Holy Ghost. God has given us everything we need for life and godliness, and Scripture tells us it comes through knowing Jesus, the One who calls us to glory and virtue (II Peter 1:3).

A girl's heart should be so lost in God, a guy must seek Him to find her.

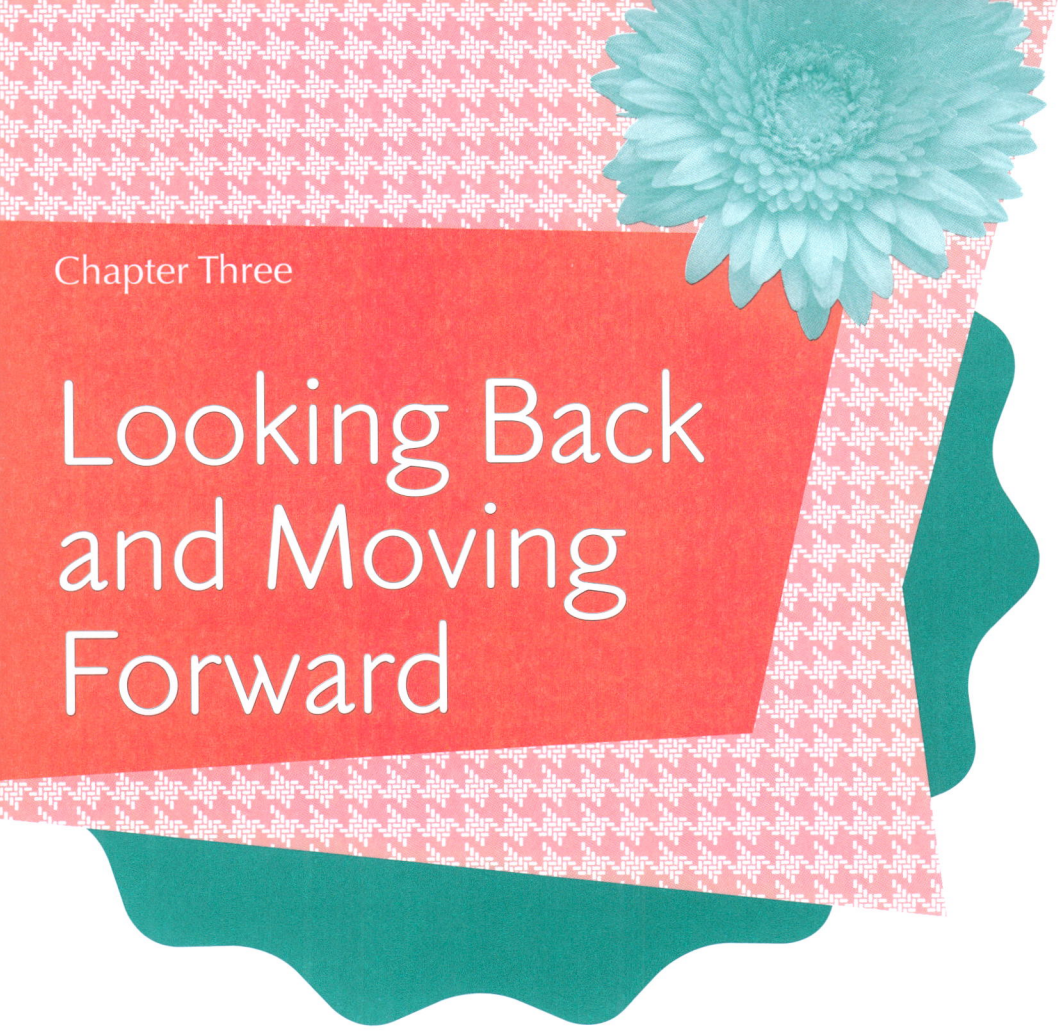

Chapter Three

Looking Back and Moving Forward

The way things are is not the way they always were. If you've seen pictures depicting America a century ago, I'm sure you noticed a huge difference in the way people dressed, interacted, and lived.

In his book, *How America Lost Her Innocence: A History of the Sexual Revolution*, Steve Gallagher documents the fall of morality in our nation. Much of the information following summarizes his findings.

Alfred Kinsey, born in 1894, is credited with being the "father of the sexual revolution." Raised in a Christian home, Kinsey later became a devoted atheist. Educated in the field of zoology, Kinsey began conducting "research" in a field now called "sexology." Funded by the Rockefeller Foundation, he conducted experiments and published his "findings." His books made him a celebrity of sorts.

Although his "findings" were disturbing, of greater significance is that much of them were based on skewed information. Why do I mention this? Because I believe it's important for you to know that much of what is taught in today's sex ed classes is based on Kinsey's "studies" and "experiments."

According to Gallagher, Kinsey gathered skewed data and presented it as being reliable. For instance, information he said was received from various sources was actually obtained from one man, a child abuser. Dr. Judith Reismen, a researcher and expert witness in sex science, said of Kinsey's findings, "Children have been tortured for this so-called scientific data."[2]

Kinsey was fascinated with any kind of sexual deviancy. He had a particular interest in what happened in the minds of people who, for "pleasure," hurt themselves and others, including children. He set up a studio in his home and filmed things no one should ever do or watch. Why did people listen to this man who built his theories on Darwin's ideas that people were much the same as animals and they should not restrain themselves from any sexual urges?

Roughly 86 percent of the people interviewed by Kinsey (who claimed he was sampling the average American) were discovered to be from a pool of prisoners, homosexual activists, pimps, thieves, and prostitutes. To make his research look more viable, he gave the title "married women" to prostitutes. This is the man American academics look to for "scientific research" in regards to human sexuality, and whose work continues to influence our social and cultural values.

Based on Kinsey's research, child molesters could justify themselves into thinking they were doing something nice for their victims. In one book published in 1953, he claimed that no real harm was done to the over four thousand rape victims interviewed.

May I suggest that perhaps we would do better to look to the Word of God instead of a lust-filled bisexual man who lived in an "open" marriage with his wife? Unlike Kinsey's theory that promoted the idea that delaying sexual experience is harmful to people, what does the Creator of humanity and sexuality say on the subject?

Before we go on, I would like to give you just a little more information on who is behind what is being promoted in our society today. A branch of the Kinsey Institute was established in 1964 by a former medical director of Planned Parenthood. Their goal was to promote Kinsey's findings to children. This venture was funded not only by the Kinsey Institute, but also received a big grant from the Playboy Foundation.

Their tactic was to persuade teachers and academic leaders that experts should present information on sexuality and that it should be from a scientific point of view, not a moral one. Among their goals was to gain acceptance for things moral societies have never tolerated, things I don't feel comfortable repeating here. If you are old enough or have your parents' permission, I recommend reading *How America Lost Her Innocence: A History of the Sexual Revolution*, by Steve Gallagher.

> Things have definitely gone downhill since Kinsey's fake "studies" were accepted by those with "itching ears" (or other itching body parts). Kinsey's lies gave "information" that corrupt men wanted to hear and that launched a porn business that has escalated into a multi-billion dollar industry. Some estimate that pornography produces an annual income greater than football, baseball, and basketball combined.[3] That's a lot of money!

THE KINSEY FALLOUT

What has our nation gained as a result of the sexual revolution? Yes, people were "freed" from their "old-fashioned" moral values. In reality, they have taken on a new bondage that has caused tremendous pain and even death. You've probably passed a building where inside people are engaged in watching things, even participating in things that are controlling their lives. Exotic dancing, X-rated movies, books and magazines, even prostitution all involve not only sexual sin but are laced with drug use and despair. The devil has twisted pure love, what God meant to give men and women pleasure, into something sick, demoralizing, and unsatisfying.

In our Western society, culture seems to scream at our kids, "If it feels good to you, then it must be all right." With the motive to satisfy its own lusts, modern society has promoted a doctrine called "moral relativism." Those who believe in this philosophy think there is no absolute right or wrong and that what one person sees as evil another might see as good. In this school of thought, good and evil are determined by an individual's perspective—and no one person's perspective should be forced on someone else.

Moral relativists deny the existence of a God who will ultimately determine their eternal destinies. With that as their foundation, they feel free to do whatever they want without concern for the consequences their actions might have on another person. What's important to them is what satisfies their desires, without regard for the possible destruction their actions might bring.

My friend, that is not true. That is not right. That is not loving.

THE PROCESS AND PROGRESSION OF PURITY

We've seen the progressive slide of immorality. Let's look now at the process and progression of purity.

Not one of us was born pure, but God, through the blood of Jesus, makes us innocent. The blood of Jesus is the cleansing agent that separates us from our sin (I John 1:7). He fills us with His Spirit, which enables us to walk a pure path as we cooperate with His leading.

Ultimately, it is in God's purpose to transform our character. If we look clean on the outside, but inside we are filthy, we aren't clean. If the Lord has given us a clean heart on the inside, we need to reflect that on the outside in the ways we present and conduct ourselves. We aren't clean or pure if we are only clean on the inside or the outside. We must have both.

On our journey of purity, we may mess up along the way. God knows that and has already committed to love us regardless of our slip-ups. He will restore us if we renew our commitment to Him.

| **It's up to us to fight for purity.** | Walk outside on a rainy day and see if your shoes get muddy.

They will! Living in this world, we will come in contact with things that have the same "muddying" effect on our hearts, minds, and spirits. This is why we are told in James 4:8 to purify our hearts, to cleanse ourselves. Dirt happens. It comes with breathing in this old world.

Jesus said, "Blessed are the pure in heart: for they shall see God" (Matthew 5:8). I want to see Jesus, don't you?

In his famous devotional, *My Utmost for His Highest*, Oswald Chambers wrote that purity is much more than innocence. He said: "Purity is the result of continued spiritual harmony with God. We have to grow in purity. Our life with God may ... become spotted and stained. God intentionally does not protect us from this possibility, because this is the way we recognize the need to maintain our spiritual vision through personal purity."

Did you notice the connection between a pure heart and spiritual vision? Mr. Chambers went on to encourage people to keep their "inner sanctuary" right with God as well as their "outer courts." His point was that in order to maintain our close relationships with God, there are some things we simply must not do.

With that in mind, we must acknowledge that none of us can purify our own hearts from sin (Proverbs 20:9). There simply is no real purity outside of God. Jesus "gave himself for us, that he might redeem us from all iniquity, and purify unto himself a peculiar people, zealous of good works" (Titus 2:14).

Once a person is born again with a pure heart, it's her job to help protect it. God gives the gift, and we must help maintain it. If your parents gave you a new car and you didn't keep oil in the engine, it wouldn't last long. If we aren't careful to maintain purity, the pull of the world will surely have its effect. Think of it this way. You could spend all day getting your room so clean you could eat off the floor. I love the feeling of clean, don't you? If you shut that bedroom door and didn't come back for a year, would you still be able to eat off that floor? Only if you like the taste of dust, I'd say.

I want you to get this. There is a cleaning only God can do for us (Isaiah 4:3-4), and there's a cleaning that is our responsibility (Isaiah 1:16). The best scrubbing agent for spiritual uncleanness is a good washing in the Word of God.

Chapter Four

Heart Start

As I thought on the ways we are supposed to love the Lord, I wondered if there was a significance in the order the Lord presented His great command. The very first thing He said was to love the Lord your God with all your heart. It seems this must be the very beginning.

In the Bible, the heart has to do with the source of our thoughts, attitudes, desires, character, and motivation. In the Hebrew, the heart is closely connected to our minds. In the New Testament, in the Greek language, mind and heart are both mentioned (Mark 12:30; Luke 10:27). Regardless of which testament we look at, the primary thing the Lord mentions first is the very core of who we are—our attitudes, motivations, and desires.

> ## "Keep your heart with all diligence, for out of it spring the issues of life"
> **(Proverbs 4:23, NKJV).**

If we are "keeping" our hearts, that implies a process. Yes, there is a moment we are born again, but we remain very human. Every person filled with God's Spirit still has flesh to deal with. The apostle Paul, someone I consider a strong Christian, dealt with human weaknesses (Romans 7:13-17). He wrote that the flesh and the Spirit are contrary to one another (Galatians 5:17). The *Common English Version* puts it this way: "A person's selfish desires are set against the Spirit, and the Spirit is set against one's selfish desires. They are opposed to each other, so you shouldn't do whatever you want to do."[4]

Do your desires line up with God's purpose and plan for your life? He longs to give His followers abundant blessings and fullness of joy. So allow your dreams to be conformed to the Lord's will, and follow His guidance faithfully. Only when you surrender to Him will you experience God's best for your life.

It's not something we really like to think about, but "the heart is deceitful above all things, and desperately wicked: who can know it?" (Jeremiah 17:9). My heart? Your heart? Wicked? Surely not! The Bible is confronting us with a harsh reality. It's possible that we do not know how off track our own thoughts and feelings can be at times. That's why it's so important to stay in the Word of God.

WORK IN PROCESS

Heart purity is a joint work in process. God plays His part, and we also share responsibility. Paul hits us hard and included himself when he said, "Dearly beloved, let us cleanse ourselves from all filthiness of the flesh and spirit" (II Corinthians 7:1).

Did you see there is both filthiness of the flesh and spirit? Did you notice that we are supposed to cleanse ourselves from both of these? We are responsible to clean house of anything that would contaminate our bodies or spirits.

- We can't allow evil thoughts to "lodge within" us (Jeremiah 4:14).
- We must speak truth, look straight ahead, and consider the paths where our feet are taking us (Proverbs 4:24-26).
- If we want to stand in God's holy place with Him, we must be committed to keeping clean hands, pure hearts, and honest words (Psalm 24:3-4).
- We've got to have "truth in the inward parts" (Psalm 51:6).

When our hearts are right with God, His blessings are with us. When we aren't double-minded, we have peace and stability. When our motives are pure, we won't be ashamed. If, however, God is dealing with you about an area in your life, then I encourage you to deal with it as well. The Lord's motive is not to shame you but to cleanse you.

One story in the Bible gives me a lot of hope. You've probably heard about the woman caught in a sexual sin. Jesus gave her mercy, and then what did He say? "Go and sin no more."

Do you think the Lord really thought this woman would never commit any sin ever again? He was telling her not to choose a lifestyle of sin. God knows our hearts. If we stumble along the way, we just need to get up and get right.

Everyone has impure thoughts at one time or another. The issue is not whether we have them but whether we entertain them.

We can only pursue purity in faith, knowing our efforts alone are not enough. Instead we trust that God will be faithful to complete what He has begun in us (Philippians 1:6). When we submit to the work of God in our lives, we reveal our true love for Him.

If I can get you to grasp one concept in this section, I want you to get this: When Jesus forgives us and washes our sins away in the waters of baptism then fills us with His Spirit, He restores us to right relationship with God. He gives us His righteousness, and that means we are counted as innocent before God. That does not mean we will never have another impure thought, but we are called to grow in grace and pursue holiness in this new relationship with God.

We are walking on a path *with* Jesus *into* purity that begins and must be maintained in the heart.

PURE HEART

Loving and pleasing God may be everything you're living for. If that's the case, consider this a checkup. Like a nurse sticks a thermometer in a patient's mouth, let's look into our hearts and see what the temperature is inside.

When the Bible speaks of loving the Lord with all of our hearts, it is referring to the center of all our physical and spiritual lives. It's talking about the "inner person." The word for "heart" is also translated "midst" which means the middle, center, or core of who we are.[5]

"Heart" also refers to our brains. Let me give you a couple of Scripture verses for that.

> **"O Jerusalem, wash your heart from wickedness, that you may be saved. How long shall your evil thoughts lodge within you?"**
> **(Jeremiah 4:14, NKJV).**

> **"For out of the heart proceed evil thoughts"**
> **(Matthew 15:19, NKJV).**

From these verses, it's clear that a heart is more than just the place emotions live. The human heart has been described as a "fountain" of "thoughts, passions, desires, appetites, affections, purposes, endeavors."[6]

According to the *Jewish Encyclopedia*, the human heart is the "seat of emotional and intellectual life" and has three main functions: knowing, feeling, and willing.[7]

You and I were made to love God. Augustine, a theologian from long ago, said these words that are still true today: "You have made us for yourself, and our heart is restless until it rests in you."⁸ There's just something in us that is never completely satisfied until we know the Lord.

ENLARGED HEART

In Psalm 119:32, the Bible implies that God can "enlarge" our hearts. That means to widen or make like a roomy pasture. There's always more of God to be had. The question is this: Is there room in our hearts?

Honestly, the answer will always be "there could be more," and that's OK. That doesn't mean we're wickedly evil and on the path to destruction. It just means we're human. That's why it's good to pray, "Search me, O God, and know my heart: try me, and know my thoughts: And see if there be any wicked way in me, and lead me in the way everlasting" (Psalm 139:23-24).

Self-examination is a good thing. We should ask the Lord to search and test our hearts. It's not always fun, but it's in our best interest when He shows us areas that need improving.

A TEACHABLE HEART

To be pure in heart, we have to be submitted to God's teaching and correction. Again, this doesn't mean the Lord isn't pleased with us as we are growing. It's a daily trading in of our hearts' desires for His. That's repentance.

Repentance is the foundation of any relationship with God. It's not just something we do one day, but it's a lifestyle we live. Daily we need to change our views and purposes to accept the will of God deep in the core of who we are. In a sense, it is a giving of ourselves to Him.

A SURRENDERED HEART

It encourages me to read in Psalm 119:1 that when we walk in the ways of the Lord, we are blameless (NIV). Continuing in this psalm, as we learn, we should obey (vv. 7-8); and the end result is that we will not be put to shame (v. 6).

Doesn't it give you hope to know that we can change? That our lives can bring glory and not reproach to the Lord?

When it comes to our hearts, there's one key verse I hope you will memorize and cherish:

> "Thy word have I hid in mine heart, that I might not sin against thee" (Psalm 119:11).

In order to know if how we are living is pleasing God, we must know His Word. The word "hid" actually means treasure. Hiding the Word in our hearts is more than just being able to recite hundreds of verses. Do we treasure the content, the message in those verses? Because they come from the One we love?

The first verse I memorized after I became a believer was II Timothy 2:15: "Study to shew thyself approved unto God, a workman that needeth not to be ashamed, rightly dividing the word of truth."

I used to think I needed to study the Bible so God would approve of me, but what this verse really means is that we study the Word so we can learn how to rightly apply it. When we understand God's Word, we live in ways that won't make us ashamed. "Blessed are they that keep his testimonies, and that seek him with the whole heart" (Psalm 119:2).

When it comes to hiding the Word in our hearts, I really like the UPCI Bible Quizzing program's theme: Learn it. Love it. Live it. We need to practice all three!

HEART MEASURES

We've laid some good groundwork, but let's dig a little deeper. Hearts aren't surface level, after all. The true measure of a person is their heart character. Character is revealed in a person's conduct and is a product of what they believe and treasure.

> "God never measures the mind. He always puts His tape measure in the heart."
> ~ Corrie ten Boom

When it comes to relationships, it's normal for a girl to think some guy is totally adorable. Every girl wonders what it would be like to have a boyfriend. It's natural to think about marriage and romance. God gave us emotions, and there is nothing wrong with them. We just need to make sure they don't monopolize our lives.

The Bible says to set our affections on things above (Colossians 3:2). Love what is eternal most. It's not only the Bible way to live, it's the best way. If you haven't done it yourself, you probably know someone who gave her heart to someone who didn't love her back. There are girls who set themselves up to experience heartache after heartache. I want better than that for you.

As relationships progress emotionally, a desire for physical intimacy is a natural response. That's when it's really important to be careful, not just go with the flow. We can't let desire override what we know to be the best choices for our lives. I'll give you an example. Sometimes girls just want to be held, but that's not safe, my friend.

We're talking about purity, and we're talking about heart. I believe the Lord wants you to protect your heart from emotional scars by not getting involved in scads of different relationships. It can be very hard on a person when they have several emotionally intimate relationships that end in disappointment. I've said it before, and I'll say it again: playing games with someone's heart is no fun, even when it's your own heart. And while we're on the subject, try not to go too fast in a relationship and make a quick commitment you might be sorry for later.

HEART SAFETY

If you want to live a pure life, here's some proactive advice found in Proverbs 4:23 (NIV):

"Above all else, guard your heart, for everything you do flows from it."

Danish philosopher Sorin Kierkegaard said, "Purity of heart is to will one thing and that thing is Jesus." When loving and pleasing God fills our hearts, we have a filter in our lives that keeps contaminates away.

When it comes to heart matters, things like humility and pure motives are of the utmost importance. Everything starts in the heart, including physical purity. If we don't guard our hearts, we may find ourselves being controlled by our emotions or even other people.

I'll let you in on one of my regular prayers. I pray this all the time: "Jesus, purify my heart, my mind, my emotions, my motives." Our flesh tempts us, our minds "think us" into things, and Satan is always looking for an access point. Allow God to change any aspect of your ambition that is not His will.

I know it sounds almost military, but we really can't afford to let our guard down. Above all else, we must guard our hearts.

Remember David's prayer in Psalm 51:10: "Create in me a clean heart, O God." If you sincerely, fervently ask God for a pure heart, He's going to give it to you! He wants to give it to you! He went to Calvary to give it to you! Pray with faith, believing!

PURE HEARTS = PURE CONDUCT

Physical purity is a big concern, but to be honest, when we concentrate more on what our flesh is doing than what is in our hearts, we really have things backwards. Our outward conduct is the last to reveal serious inner issues.

Our hearts should be ruled by the peace of God (Colossians 3:15). When we're walking close with the Lord, the Holy Ghost is not going to ignore you getting ready to fall off a spiritual cliff. He's going to let you know when you're about to make a wrong choice, and He'll give you peace when you're going the right way. Oh, it's a great way to live! When your conduct is in agreement with the Spirit in you and the Word of God, the result is pure delight.

> **"The statutes of the LORD are right, rejoicing the heart: the commandment of the LORD is pure, enlightening the eyes"**
> **(Psalm 19:8).**

PURE RUBBISH

A word of warning: Be careful that your pursuit for purity doesn't create a stumbling block of false superiority. That's like saying, "I'm so proud that I'm humble." It just doesn't work.

On the other hand, we have to be careful we aren't living a double life, pretending we are pure by outer appearances and public conduct, while all the while inside we have very impure thoughts and motives. That's a path of chaos, not blessing. What does the Bible say about serving two masters? It just doesn't work.

Remember, blessed are the pure in heart! They have a great reward: seeing God (Matthew 5:8). Yes, that's a promise of Heaven, but I believe it is for now, too. God is not hiding. He wants to be seen. Looking for the key to open the door? It's a pure heart.

> He who serves two masters has to lie to one.

PURE LOVE

Having a pure heart shows how we love God—faithfully—like a husband and wife. If you were married, you wouldn't be flirting with someone else. You wouldn't kiss a married man. We get that. Time and time again, the Bible links unfaithfulness to idolatry. To truly love and serve God, we have to be faithful to Him in our hearts and in our everyday choices in the same way a married girl is to her guy.

One of my favorite verses about making choices, especially the big decisions, is Isaiah 60:17. Several years ago I read this in the original 1984 NIV translation, and it's the last part of the verse I want to look at: "I will make peace your governor and righteousness your ruler."

What is a governor? It's a head of state, a decision maker. I don't know about you, but I can get into lots of states: states of confusion, states of distress. Whatever state I'm in, I need to let the peace of God be my top decision maker.

The word "righteousness" here is talking about our motivations—literally, our task master. What makes me do what I do? If the motive is what is righteous, and I have the peace of God confirming the way to go, that's how I make decisions, large and small. In a nutshell, to live in true purity of heart, we have to learn to continually say "yes" to God and "no" to anything that would separate us from Him—from big, dark, ugly sin to something as small as a distraction. We know we are supposed to hate evil (Romans 12:9), but in our world today, depending on who we are listening to, we might question why this is right and that is wrong. Satan specializes in presenting us with opportunities for instant gratification while promising us that giving in to our fleshly desires will bring us the satisfaction we seek.

Because of our fleshly weaknesses, our desires need to be controlled. Paul compared the Christian life to that of athletes who are so focused on winning the race that they exercise self-control in every area of their lives. That's exactly how we're called to live, yet we lack the motivation, determination, and power to do so in our own strength. For this reason, we need to rely on the Spirit of God within us. If we yield our lives to Him and step out in obedience to His promptings, we'll have the strength to say no when fleshly desires feel overpowering (Galatians 5:16).

> Keep our focus on the eternal instead of the here and now.

The key is keeping our focus on the eternal instead of the here and now. When the enemy tempts us, he tries to keep our attention on our desire and the pleasure of indulgence rather than on the eternal rewards and blessings we're giving up. Just remind yourself how quickly immediate gratification wanes and how long eternity lasts.

Holy "convictions" can't come from a corrupt source. The Bible will always trump what you, me, your health teacher, the media, or your best buddy thinks.

HEART TO HEART

It's so important to keep closely connected with the Lord. I'm not talking about having a "prayer life," but living your life in God's presence. More than reading a devotion each day, you can live devoted to the One Who made you and gave Himself for you. Purity is keeping your heart close to God's.

When we walk closely with the Lord, the world may still have some appeal, but we won't fall as easily for its attractions. Why? Because we know who we are and whose we are. I want to walk so close to God there is no room for anyone or anything to come between us. When it's time to think about having a relationship with a guy, I want you to look for that kind of passion and purity. If your "person of interest" is walking close to God, and you are walking close to God—wow! That could be something beautiful!

PURE UGLY

Have you ever met someone who was so consumed with themselves it just about made you sick? I know, we're supposed to think good thoughts about everyone, but sometimes it's hard. | **You know when it's the worst? When we find that person in the mirror.** |

Jesus offers abundant life, freedom from sin, joy unspeakable, and so much more. Walking with the Lord is the best life ever. We are called, as we walk with Him, to follow His example. There are some amazing, wonderful promises written for us in the New Testament. There are some really hard things, too.

The apostle Paul said he died daily. He wasn't talking about losing a life on a video game. He was talking about exchanging his personal desires to live out God's desires for him. Just imagine how much of the New Testament would be missing if Paul chose to live selfishly.

Paul could have let his emotions make his decisions for him. There were times he knew in advance that when he was going somewhere he would be imprisoned, beaten, and even killed. He went anyway.

When we look at the great picture of our lives, emotions last only a moment. Yes, emotions are God-given and powerful. They can draw us closer to God or turn our attention away from Him. We just can't let them boss us around. Say this out loud:

"Emotions, you're not the boss of me!"

Here's a pure heart tip: When emotions are raging, it's best to wait on any decision making. We don't want temporary feelings to lead us into decisions that could affect us long term, possibly for eternity.

> "Purity in the heart is like medicine in the body, it expels disease."
> ~ *The Homiletic Review*, 1896

THE MOUTH SPEAKS

Pure words are the natural outflow of a pure heart. They lack contaminants and reveal the character of their speaker.

We wouldn't expect both fresh and salt water to come from the same fountain, would we? (See James 3:11.) Neither should blessing and cursing come from the same lips. Your lips and mine were meant to bless and encourage, not spew out verbal vomit.

If our inner person is pure, our words should be, too. There's just one little problem—a "little member" that gets us into big trouble. Our tongues! James said the person who keeps his tongue from offending anyone is the same as a perfect man (James 3:2). Those who keep their tongues from sinning have the ability to keep their whole bodies sin-free!

Here's another great verse: "A good man out of the good treasure of his heart bringeth forth that which is good; and an evil man out of the evil treasure of his heart bringeth forth that which is evil: for of the abundance of the heart his mouth speaketh" (Luke 6:45). These are Jesus' words, and He was telling His followers that their inner person overflows into the world around them by the words they speak.

When we love God, we will hide His Word in our hearts so that we might not sin against Him (Psalm 119:11). The law of God teaches, and the love of God constrains, or keeps us together (II Corinthians 5:14)—even our lips, when necessary.

WHAT NOT TO SAY

It's probably not a big surprise to you that the Bible has some things to say about the things we say. Let's look at some verses.

> "Keep thy tongue from evil, and thy lips from speaking guile" (Psalm 34:13).
>
> "But fornication, and all uncleanness, or covetousness, let it not be once named among you, as becometh saints; neither filthiness, nor foolish talking, nor jesting, which are not convenient: but rather giving of thanks" (Ephesians 5:3-4).

These verses tell us that sexual immorality, impurity, and greed should not even be mentioned in conversation among God's people. The NIV puts it this way: "There must not be even a hint of sexual immorality, or of any kind of impurity."

Paul also wrote in Ephesians 4:29, "Let no corrupt communication proceed out of your mouth, but that which is good to the use of edifying, that it may minister grace unto the hearers." The words "corrupt communication" refer to unwholesome talk, and those are things we ought not to say.

> ### "Filthy talk makes us feel comfortable with filthy action."
> ### ~ Clement of Alexandria

Paul gives us godly counsel, but it's not always easy to apply in the day-to-day of life. When girls start dissing on dating, our ears just perk up. And if it's our guy, well, we just love to talk about him, don't we? If your heart can't handle holding it in, just remember to keep the conversation clean!

When it comes to guys, it's a big mistake to start talking about physical desires with them, especially if it's someone you are in a relationship with. It will only stir things up. When people start talking about intimate things, it activates their brains to engage in thoughts and conversations that actually release chemicals that cause strong desires for intimacy.

PURE WORDS

"The words of the L<small>ORD</small> are pure words"
(Psalm 12:6).

"The thoughts of the wicked are an
abomination to the L<small>ORD</small>:
but the words of the pure are pleasant words"
(Proverbs 15:26).

"Thy word is very pure:
therefore thy servant loveth it"
(Psalm 119:140).

An Iranian poet said, "The words you speak become the house you live in." **Not only do the words we hear affect us, so also do the words we speak!** Sometimes we may scream them, but more often they are inner voices that replay messages over and over. We should pray the words of King David: "Let the words of my mouth, and the meditation of my heart, be acceptable in thy sight, O L<small>ORD</small>, my strength, and my redeemer" (Psalm 19:14).

IN OTHERS' WORDS

I have a question. How come the people who know the least about God's Word are often the ones who want to tell folks the most about it? They say things like, "Well, I think . . ." and "I believe . . ." and "God couldn't mean . . . ." We need to make sure the words we listen to are legit. No matter the medium, is the message rooted in the truth?

People, some with good intentions, and some not, attempt to influence others to their opinions. With that in mind, I wrote this little rhyme:

If God controls the inner you, the world can't tell you what to do!

Don't allow yourself to be polluted by listening to garbage. Polluted words are not pure. And while we are on the subject, may I advise you not to listen to any junk spoken against your pastor or leaders. They can dull your spiritual hearing and affect your ability to be ministered to.

God wants to lead you in His ways. The key is keeping "in" the way, on the path. Keep listening to good preaching and teaching, attending services and classes, and hiding God's Word in your heart. The Hebrew word for "hid" means to store God's Word like a treasure. When God's girls treasure His

Word, the beautiful truths found there displace the words of the world, the enemy, and our carnal natures.

THE WORD AT YOUR FINGERTIPS

Social media can be a wonderful tool. It's a great way to connect with friends and family all over the world. It also has its downside. Social media provides the opportunity for people to talk about things they would be afraid to discuss in public or in a one-on-one relationship. Be aware of the false sense of security the "screen" brings. And remember that, like your picture, your words can go viral with just a couple of clicks.

GOD'S WORDS

"My sheep hear my voice, and I know them, and they follow me" (John 10:27).

We are receptors, constantly picking up signals around us. We read words. We hear words. We sing words and say words. Choose carefully what you "tune in" to, purposefully limiting exposure to places and people you know affect you in negative ways. When it's your choice, choose to go places and hang with friends that build you up! Remember, God's girls are supposed to love what is sincere, hate what is evil, and cling to what is good (Romans 12:9).

TESTIMONY

My mom was so great. When I was growing up, she never talked about virginity, but purity. I can remember her saying a thousand times that you lose purity long before you lose virginity. She made it clear that purity wasn't just about physical nature, but language, what you watched, etc.

She made me realize that it was important for me to decide what "pure" was and what "crossed the line."

I have a lot of concern that the "but everyone's doing it" mentality has been accepted even in church. People that I go to church with think it's normal to move in together. I understand that by the standards of our world, people do this, but according to the Word of God, it's still wrong, regardless of what society says.

I was married just last year. It was a long wait. I was thirty-two, and my husband and I were both virgins. That was important to me, and when I made it important, that is what I got. The rewards are worth the wait.

~ Sarah Hogan

My friend Natalie shared her condensed, twelve-word summary of Psalm 78 to help us with our words:

"A testimony on the lips will keep temptation out of the heart!"
~ Natalie Jordan

Chapter Five

Pure Vision

A Yiddish proverb says, "The eyes are the mirror of the soul." This wise saying lets us know that the things we focus on 1) *reflect* what's in our hearts, and 2) *affect* what's in our hearts.

We've looked at Matthew 5:8: "Blessed are the pure in heart: for they will see God." Seeing God is incredibly important. I believe to have good spiritual vision, we need to protect what we are looking at with our natural eyes.

When the Word says, "turn … from beholding vanity" (Psalm 119:37), it is referring to focusing on things that are empty, vain, or worthless. If we're taught to avoid those things, it's pretty clear we should not be looking at nasty stuff.

I hope every girl reading this book realizes that watching things that provoke or awaken impure thoughts is flat out wrong. Christians are supposed to separate themselves from sin, not be entertained by it.

If the movies you watch, the television you see, and the music you listen to keep flashing images and word pictures about sex, guess what you will be focused on? Duh. Please make sure you are not watching scenes that stir up desires in you that should not be fulfilled outside of marriage.

I promise you, Christian young lady, that if you give in to sexual temptation, it is not going to be like what you have seen in a movie or television show. If you are trying

> If you give in to sexual temptation, it is not going to be like what you have seen in a movie or television show.

to walk with God, your actions will cause you to be plagued with guilt and shame—and it's also very likely your actions will set your feet on a path you don't want to walk down.

So many times sexual activity does the opposite of what a girl hopes for. It doesn't cement a relationship; it is the beginning of the end of a relationship. Once a girl feels "used," it becomes easier to give herself to someone else, and then someone else. There's a void that longs to be filled, and so many times, in the trying to fill it, girls instead find themselves lost, far from God, pregnant, infected, or worse. Even good Christian girls who have made these types of mistakes have become so distraught they attempted suicide or turned to drugs.

Yes, Jesus is waiting to forgive and restore, but so many times injured and disillusioned girls feel unworthy or become so hardened they just don't turn to Him. The emptiness leads people to try more, do more. Those who eventually turn to the Lord and become restored pay a heavy price for their choices.

Don't look around you for fulfillment. Look up!

When we look around, we see the undeniable truth that the values in our nation are crumbling. Did you know that a sexual scene occurs on television five times every hour, but up to 6.7 times every hour in the top teen shows?[9] The average child spends more than fifty-three hours a week with media.

Between phones, computers, tablets, TVs, and other electronic devices, young people are immersed in media much of their days. What is projected onscreen is most often not produced by godly, Bible-believing people. Most of what is played does not encourage purity of any kind: emotional, spiritual, or sexual. It's up to you to filter what you see and hear. Think about it this way.

What you watch is programming your thoughts.

We are supposed to be thinking about things that are pure, lovely, and of a good report. We want these things to program our thoughts, right? If we are watching things that hinder us from being more and more Christ-like, we are missing the boat.

> "Indeed, what would one search for when one has God before one's eyes?
> Or what would satisfy one who would not be satisfied with God?"
> ~ *Augustine*

SELF-VISION

When we turn our eyes on the Lord, we will see many of our struggles shrink and ultimately vanish. When our focus is on Jesus, we not only get a beautiful vision of Him, we get an accurate vision of our worth to Him.

When you see your value as God sees your value, your world can turn right-side-up! In both your appearance and your conduct, you will hold yourself to a higher standard. Think of it this way: You aren't like a greasy take-out wrapper from a fast food joint. You are more like your grandma's good china—valuable and special.

God wants His girls of faith to remember they are His precious children even on "bad hair" and "bad hormone" days! We all have days we feel like failures (inside and out), but that doesn't mean we are! Remember, we can't let our hormones and emotions boss us around.

Many times girls give themselves away easily because they don't have a right perspective on their value. When you receive the Holy Ghost in your life, you are sealed with God's approval. He

Valuable & Special

says, "She's good enough for me!" If you're good enough for Him, you're good enough for anyone!

Knowing how much you are loved and valued by God will empower you to live a pure life! No one can make you feel inferior without your consent. Don't agree with garbage.

If you are insecure about your attractiveness or your value as a person, please wait to get in a relationship. You need to learn the value of yourself first! Don't let your insecurities make you settle for less than God's child deserves!

> "The real ornament of woman is her character, her purity."
> ~ Mahatma Gandhi

THE NAKED TRUTH ABOUT PORNOGRAPHY

I hope this comes as a surprise to you, but even young girls can get addicted to pornography. Watching and reading pornography develops sexual urges and behaviors that disrupt people's lives no matter their age. Although some consider pornography a harmless pastime, in reality, it is a terrible threat to the beauty of marital intimacy.

Today, at very young ages, most boys and girls have regular access to smart phones and computers. At any moment, without constant supervision, a child could be just a click away from crud. While surfing the Web, in all innocence, with one click, many are carried away on a wave of pornography into a sea of sickness and sin.

> **"There is an interaction between seeing and being. The kind of person you are affects the kind of world that you see ... And conversely, what you see affects what you are."**
> *~ Simon Tugwell*

Statistics tell us that between 70 and 80 percent of teen boys watch pornography. When this happens, obscene smut becomes their "sex instructor." Pornography doesn't give pictures of normal relationships. It is fake, a counterfeit, and misleading. It can actually build expectations to unreachable levels that can ultimately damage relationships that were meant to be sacred. It is destructive because it builds false confidence and presents possibilities that aren't connected with real life or real people with real bodies. Hardcore porn often includes scenes of violence and abuse.

Pornography is damaging in so many ways. The truth is that it cheapens what God made beautiful. In a marriage relationship, intimacy is about a husband and wife giving themselves to each other. Pornography is selfish. In a relational sense, it bonds the user to an unreal image; but God designed physical intimacy to bond one woman and one man together for life in a wholesome, healthy way. Honoring the sacredness of God's sacred gift honors the Gift Giver.

Pornography dishonors God's plan for marital intimacy.

We can't really understand the negative effects of pornography until we understand the goodness of the pure intimacy God designed (Hebrews 13:4). We were not blessed with the gift of sight to waste our vision watching people engage in what was meant to be a private act between a husband and wife.

Shelly Lubben, a former porn actress, said the women who were porn actresses hated what they were doing so much they vomited between scenes. People watching think they love what they are doing, but they don't. They feel dehumanized and degraded by what Lubben called "repulsive acts." Of one girl's suicide, she said, "We're traumatized little girls living on anti-depressants, drugs and alcohol acting out our pain in front of you who continue to abuse us."[10] Wow. That's incredibly sad.

If people could see what goes on behind the scenes of the pornography industry, I think they would be shocked by the levels of drug and alcohol use, addictions, suicides, abuse, and more all in the name of "sexual entertainment." As for the one who watches pornography, it's a trap for them, too.

TESTIMONY

I was raised in an Apostolic Pentecostal family. My heritage is rich and I carried that with pride. I was the "perfect" Pentecostal. At least everyone would have assumed that of me, even my closest friends. However, I had a secret, and a big one: pornography—and all that came along with it.

Sexual appetites were awakened in me at an early age by no fault of my own. A "friend" of the family abused me. This activated desires that, at the time, I wasn't equipped to conquer. Initially, viewing pornography began by accident. I was chatting with a guy online. He wanted to video chat, and I innocently accepted. After a few minutes, I closed the computer. Curiosity was the motivator after that. Dear friends, curiosity may not "kill the cat," but it destroyed my innocence. I fell into the snare that was laid for me and was too ashamed to ask for help. No matter how hard I tried, or how hard I prayed, I was stuck. So, for a while, I became a beautiful Pentecostal shell of a person, deceiving others—even myself.

One night I had a dream—and it shook me to the core of all I was. I woke up afraid, convicted, and desiring to be real. I had already tried to change, but all of my strength couldn't do it. I needed help. So, I went to a friend in ministry who would maintain confidence, yet help me find a way out. Even in my sin and shame, she loved me. She exemplified the love of Christ.

By the grace of God, the help of a trusted friend's love and accountability, and a recommitment to honesty and integrity, I am an overcomer. I'm thankful that the Lord kept reaching for me. He was faithful, even when I wasn't.

~ Anonymous Overcomer

So many times girls happen on pornography accidentally and then get sucked in. It's sad, but I know the story of one girl this happened to. She got hooked, and then she started to do the things that being aroused can naturally lead to. She thought it was fine. She was still a virgin, but in her heart she knew her behavior was wrong.

Scripture tells us that men can think their ways are clean in their own eyes (Proverbs 16:2). People will make excuses to justify their actions, especially when they can get "technical" about "purity." People rationalize the things they are doing in secret, all the while knowing in their hearts that if it wasn't wrong, they wouldn't feel so rotten.

It's not easy to break from addiction, but it can be done! If you need help, or know someone who does, follow this plan to get and stay on track.

1. Be honest with yourself and acknowledge to yourself that you have a problem.
2. Trust God. He really wants to help you. He really will!
3. Talk to someone you trust who will hold you accountable.
4. Make wise choices.
5. If you fall, go back to #1 and start over.

ME, MYSELF, AND I

With the onset of smart phones, texting, video chatting, etc., a new "opportunity" has arisen for girls to get involved in pornography from the comfort of their own homes. Some might not consider these types of activities to be pornographic, but what is the definition of *pornography*, anyway?

Pornography [pawr-**nog**-r*uh*-fee]
- writings, pictures, films, etc. designed to stimulate sexual excitement
- the production of such material

Anyone with a smart phone can be the star and producer of their own home-grown pornography. It doesn't have to be marketed or paid for to qualify as porn.

Even good girls can get drawn into the world of "sexting" to "prove their love." If you don't know the word "sexting," well, I'm glad. What it means is taking sexual/naked pictures and sending them through text messages.

Please don't send your "goodies" via text message. If a guy wants you to prove your commitment in this way, he's not worth committing to. If you feel you need to do this to get someone's attention, then that's the wrong kind of attention and it leads to the wrong kind of relationship.

The things we aren't supposed to show in public should not be shown on a device that could go public at any moment. Not only is it wrong, you know how easy it is to forward a message. Many girls have experienced ruinous results when they sent a picture to a guy and it went viral. Imagine walking through the hall of your school, church, or workplace knowing many of the guys there saw an inappropriate picture of you. Never, never, never set yourself up for this!

> **The Internet is public. Body parts are private.**

I'll just throw in my two cents here. I believe it's possible to post and share pictures that are inappropriate even if the people in them are fully clothed. I'm surprised at how many pictures I see of beautiful godly girls with their hands on their hips, shoulders thrust back in ways that push their chests forward. It's like they are saying, "Look at my figure!" Pouty lips, tilted heads, and "come hither" looks are not what godly girls should be posting on any social media. I hope you care what people think when they look at those pictures. I hope you want them to see Jesus in you, not just a collection of interesting body parts.

FOR MY YOUNGER FRIENDS

We live in a hypersexualized world. You may not be familiar with that word, but you probably know what hyperactivity is. It's abnormally active. Hypersexualized means to be unusually or excessively active in or concerned with sexual matters. Being hypersexualized at a young age robs girls of their innocent youth. It's a shame girls don't get the chance to enjoy the pleasure of just being a girl.

KAGOY

The acronym for this is KAGOY, and it stands for "kids are getting older younger." One trip to the store confirms that businesses are marketing sexuality to young girls. I didn't know this, but some dolls made for little girls to play with are sold with thong underwear! Products are developed and targeted to young girls that are unbelievably sexual—from a stripper pole (complete with money and garter) to push-up bras and thong underwear for elementary school-aged children.

Vending machines were once filled with stickers and gumballs, but now they carry "tramp stamp" temporary tattoos so little girls can have "targets" printed on their lower backs. School supplies, like pencil boxes and binders, are being made with the Playboy logo.

Girls, don't even look at this junk-junka-lona! It's garbage. Buying, wearing, or using these things is not for you! You are so much more than the object of someone's sexual desire, but we become numbed by so many images we don't realize we are tolerating what used to be shocking and is still inappropriate. This might step on toes, but even some of the shoes girls wear are called "stripper heels." We must draw the line and not associate with the ungodly in the things we do or the way we look.

CRITICAL THINKING

The word "critical" isn't always thought of in a positive light, but for our discussion, we are using it to mean skillful decision making. That sounds good, doesn't it?

Think about this with me. If girls learn what being a girl means from the things they see in their society, what are they to think? If boys learn how to treat girls by what society promotes, what will they think?

To sum it up, applying critical thinking, girls are pressured to look and act sexy; and boys are trained this is what to look for in a girl. Even the magazines at the grocery are headlined with what girls can do to catch a guy, how to look hot and satisfy her partner. It's crucial we get our views on sexuality from the Bible, not the general public. Don't allow yourself to be drawn in by society's sensual standards.

GUARD YOUR GIZZARD

I know you're not a chicken and you don't really have a gizzard, but another word for gizzard is "innards." A gizzard is in the digestive system—it's a place where things get ground up and prepared to be digested and nourish the body.

Guard what you put in your "gizzard"—your inner person—because it will affect your health and strength. I want to give you some Scripture verses to think about. I hope they encourage you.

"I made a covenant with mine eyes; why then should I think upon a maid?" (Job 31:1). This verse is from a guy's perspective, but it applies to us girls, too.

"The eye is the lamp of the body. So if your eye is sound, your entire body will be full of light. But if your eye is unsound, your whole body will be full of darkness. If then the very light in you [your conscience] is darkened, how dense is that darkness!" (Matthew 6:22-23, AMP). This verse is saying our eyes are like windows for our bodies. When we look at good things, we have all the light we need, but if we look at bad things, everything is dark. Even good things can seem bad when the light inside of us is dark.

The Lord said in Ezekiel 20:7, "Cast ye away every man the abominations of his eyes." In other words, don't be looking at disgusting stuff. Have you heard of GIGO? That means garbage in, garbage out. If we are watching shows that depict sinful activities, we are, in a sense, indulging in the pleasure of those activities. Do we dare think we won't be held accountable?

"Have no fellowship with the unfruitful works of darkness, but rather reprove them" (Ephesians 5:11). God's girls are the children of the light, and we are not to take part in things done in the dark. Instead, we are to show through the witness of our lives, how wrong they are. We are living the best life possible in the glory of God's blessings and favor. This is the good stuff!

Chapter Six

Pure Soul

"Soul" and "heart" and "mind" are often used interchangeably, and with valid reason. If you look up the definitions and try to define the lines between them, it can rattle your brain.

I spent a lot of time working on this section, studying, and praying, and searching for the right way to explain these concepts. They are important. They are who and what we are.

Before we jump into "soul," let's first look at "spirit." Spirit is the beginning, the starting point for each of us. Spirit is the breath that comes from God and will eventually go back to Him (Psalm 146:4). When God made Adam, He created a body and then He breathed life, or spirit, into him and caused him to become a "living soul." (See Genesis 2:7.)

Souls are: ═══ Rational ═══ Spiritual ═══ Emotional

I want you to close your eyes for a minute. Imagine you could look inside your body. You would see organs working, blood moving around, digestion happening. But imagine a picture of your soul in there touching every part of your inner person. What you do with your body affects your soul, and the condition of your soul can affect your body.

I don't like to look at the negative, but Psalm 88:3 tells us our souls can be filled with evil. I prefer to reverse that principle and realize instead that in the same way, my soul can be filled with good. It's up to us; we are affected by life and things that are external—and internal, like hormones. Thoughts can bombard us, but we have to know that every thought or feeling isn't from God, even though the gift of thinking and emotions are.

Below is a little chart with Scripture that shows the three functions of the soul.

Rational	Spiritual	Emotional
Souls can know. *Psalm 139:14*	**Souls can be lifted to God.** *Psalm 86:4*	**Souls can be cast down (depressed or sad).** *Psalm 42:5*
Souls can choose. *Job 7:15*	**Souls can give praise to God.** *Psalm 146:1*	**Souls can be satisfied.** *Psalm 63:5*
Souls can obey commandments. *II Kings 23:3*	**Souls come and go from a person at life/death.** *I Kings 17:21-22*	**Souls can be weary and sorrowful.** *Jeremiah 31:25*
Souls can be set (focused) in a direction. *II Kings 23:25*	**Souls belong to God.** *Ezekiel 18:4*	**Souls can be vexed (upset).** *Psalm 6:3*
Souls can hear. *Jeremiah 4:19*	**Souls can magnify the Lord.** *Luke 1:46*	**Souls hunger and thirst.** *Proverbs 27:7; Proverbs 25:25*
Souls can reason. *Luke 12:19*	**Souls live.** *Psalm 119:175*	**Souls can love.** *Song of Solomon 3:1*
Souls can be ruled over. *Romans 13:1*	**Souls are God-made.** *Jeremiah 38:16*	**Souls can grieve.** *I Samuel 30:6*
Souls record/remember. *II Corinthians 1:23*	**Souls can seek God.** *Lamentations 3:25*	**Souls can be joyful.** *Psalm 35:9*

Jesus asked a hard question in Matthew 16:26: "What shall a man give in exchange for his soul?" He didn't leave people wondering what it would take. He actually told them the answer before the question. "If any man come after me, let him deny himself, and take up his cross, and follow me" (Matthew 16:24).

Jesus is telling us that our souls will gain entrance to Heaven for eternity if, in this life, we give our souls to following Him. If we acknowledge Him here, He will acknowledge us in the life to come (Mark 8:35). I hope you have a good picture in your mind of how wonderful Heaven is really going to be. There's nothing more important than being ready for Heaven—than being saved.

YOU'RE A SOUL WOMAN

God made you in His image. John 4:24 tells us that God is a Spirit, and that includes more than we can fit into this small book, but it implies things like self-awareness. He knows who He is! "For there is one God; and there is none other but he" (Mark 12:32). He wants you to know who you are, too. Spirit also has to do with our will, our thoughts, and our intentions.

Every person has good thoughts and bad thoughts, kind emotions and raging emotions. It's not that we get a bad thought or feeling that makes us impure, but it's what we do with it. Do we entertain it, think about it, play with it? Life is like an untraveled trail with all sorts of twists and turns. Appealing activities can be detours that lead to the quicksand of sin. The only way to be sure we're walking right is to follow the One who knows the way perfectly.

The thoughts and emotions we entertain will break through and come out in our conduct. What we believe motivates us to act in certain ways—for the good or the not-so-good. These outward things that we do reveal "soul issues." I believe with all my heart that God wants you to live above what so many choose: lives of compromise. There are some things young people deal with just because they are young, but there's a time to let them go. "Flee also youthful lusts: but follow righteousness, faith, charity, peace, with them that call on the Lord out of a pure heart" (II Timothy 2:22). According to this verse, the life choices we make should come from a pure heart that is continually calling on the Lord. This is what I call being "souled" out.

PURE EMOTIONS

Purity is being and acting the same in your home as you would in a group or in the desert where no one sees what you are doing. Soul purity has to do with integrity—keeping the same character regardless of your environment. As Christians, we are called to love God's ways and hate false ways. There's no place for pretending.

Purity is being consistent in your thoughts, words, and actions. I don't know about you, but I need the Holy Ghost to help me with that! It's good I don't have to try to live in my own strength and abilities. I have God living inside, and He's the same yesterday, today, and forever. Phew! We have hope!

Soul purity is something inside that shows up on the outside. It starts by embracing the purity God gives us and then conducting ourselves with pure motives, words, and actions. It's about living a loving relationship with a pure and holy God that motivates us in ways no threats of punishment ever could.

> "He who loves with purity considers not the gift of the lover, but the love of the giver."
> ~ Thomas a Kempis

YOUR CHOICE

Scripture compares people to "vessels" or bowls in a great house. It says some of them are special and some are not. That's how it is with people, too. When a person stops doing evil and becomes a new person in Christ, they are no longer dishonorable. Their lives become holy and pleasing to God. (See II Timothy 2:20-21.)

Remember, we aren't supposed to be like the world. Paul wrote in Romans 12:1-2 that Christians should present their bodies pure and pleasing. We are not to be conformed to this world. Instead we are to renew our minds, change the way we think, and then we will know how to do what is good and pleasing to God. If we are not careful we can forget that first love we felt when we met Him. Our bodies are the temple or dwelling place of the Holy Spirit of God. It is dangerous to continue to go along with any habit that cannot stand up under the spotlight of His love.

We can't take our advice or our counsel from the ungodly. I'm guessing that's pretty important since it's in the very first psalm. The thinking of the ungodly is not based in the truth. | **When we choose to delight ourselves in the Word of God, we will prosper!** |

Chapter Seven

Pure Mind

We've touched on having a pure mind when we talked about our souls. Just to recap, our souls include not only our spirit life and seat of emotions, but also that rational thinking part.

Think of it this way: our minds are linked to our spirits, constantly transferring information. Our minds are where our consciences live—where we have that inner sense of what is right and what is wrong. Our consciences can be our friends, but we do need to remember that if we act badly long enough, our consciences can become damaged. "Unto the pure all things are pure: but unto them that are defiled and unbelieving is nothing pure; but even their mind and conscience is defiled" (Titus 1:15). This verse of Scripture lets us know just how important it is for each of us to "be renewed in the spirit of your mind" (Ephesians 4:23).

Why is all this so important? If we have bad information in our brains, it can cause deterioration in our conscience that will absolutely affect the condition of our spiritual life. We are told to let God speak to us, and then the question comes, "How do I know when God is speaking to me?" God speaks to us through our conscience and through hearing and reading His Word. It's that simple.

Brains are pretty complicated. They've been called "the final frontier," because there is so much we don't know about how they work. Brains are more than just "gray matter"—three-pound masses of nerves, neurons, and axons. They are the most complex organs in our bodies.

TRAIN YOUR BRAIN

"O that my ways were directed to keep thy statutes! Then shall I not be ashamed, when I have respect unto all thy commandments" (Psalm 119:5-6).

The Word of God was given to us to know how to find God, get right with God, and live with God and man. We need to program our brains with His Word. Psalm 32:8 tells us we should let the Lord instruct, teach, and guide us with His eye, not our limited vision. Did you know that if you keep His Word, you can have more understanding than older people who don't (Psalm 119:100)?

Our brains are shaped by our genes. Experience also plays a part. It was recently discovered that through a process called neurogenesis, new brain cells are being born throughout our lives. This lets us know that our brains really can be changed at subconscious levels. The way you think now does not have to be the way you will always think. God can make you think differently as you bring your thoughts into agreement with His Word.

Walking with God is a faith walk, but that does not mean we check our brains at the door of the church house like we hang our coats in the hall. We are supposed to use the brains God gave us. We just need to make sure our thoughts are in agreement with God's Word. If they aren't, we need to toss them out, and fast! If we hold on to wrong thoughts, we may act on them, and that would send more bad info to our brains. This is how our consciences get weakened—even to the point of being unfeeling (I Timothy 4:2).

The good news is that through the Bible, we can get our minds renewed. I've heard it said that the Holy Ghost comes into our hearts and then God evangelizes our brains. The Holy Ghost in us preaches to our brains and converts it to Christianity. Getting saved takes a moment, but from there we are called to grow in grace (II Peter 3:18). We study (II Timothy 2:15), we choose to think on pure and lovely things (Philippians 4:8), and we spend time in His presence (II Corinthians 3:18).

PURE SOURCE

When it comes to the things we allow to shape our thoughts, we need to make sure they are coming from an accurate source. It's sad to say, but often in schools across the land, teachers give unbiblical and incomplete information when it comes to sexuality and morality.

Honor your teachers, yes, but please realize that if they are promoting something that is against biblical teaching, you need to reject that information. The truth is, there is no "safe sex" outside of marriage. The fact that the students being taught this damaging theory are emotionally immature is just a starting point in a discussion that has plenty of confusion and flat-out lies.

On top of a bad "educational" system, we have an "entertainment" industry that in many ways has spiraled into soft porn. Someone told me about a new series of books called "mommy porn" being read by women who would never go into an "adult" book store. What has inspired them to buy erotic fantasy designed to "obsess you, possess you, and stay with you forever"?

Entertainment, either in written or visual form, should not be sexually provocative or offensive. Don't pollute your mind with the wrong pictures. Think about it: *Provocative* means to stir up, arouse, or call forth (feelings, desires, or activity). It means "to incite or stimulate (a person, animal, etc.) to action." We shouldn't be doing things that we know will arouse desires that we can't yet fulfill without the blessings of marriage.

I know we already discussed pornography, but we need to make sure we don't fall into a trap of soft porn, no matter who else is reading it and saying it's fun. We need to treat all of this as poison and know, that without a doubt, there are not "fifty shades of grey" when it comes to God's Word on sexuality.

EMOTIONAL THINKING

Everyone has emotions—believers and unbelievers, alike. What makes them different in the two groups is the difference in their affections. What you care about influences your feelings, and for a Christian, our thoughts and emotions should be focused on the Lord. The affections in the heart of unbelievers are on earthly things.

Emotions are intensified thoughts. If your mind is out of control, you and your feelings are out of control.

The Holy Ghost living in you and me should have a major influence on our emotions. With our minds, we choose to cooperate with the Spirit within, as well as honor God in our life choices. As we do, our emotional health grows stronger, and healthy emotions are an important part of a healthy spiritual life. The Lord develops our lives by revealing our nature through our emotions—sadness, pain, difficulties, temptations, and such. When we follow the leading of the Spirit and the Word, we can learn to be in control of those emotions and mature as an overcomer.

> **When we follow the leading of the Spirit and the Word, we can learn to be in control of those emotions and mature as an overcomer.**

Do not allow activities or conversation in your life contrary to the Spirit or to your personal standards. The way we behave day in and day out is the best example to others of our convictions. Self-control draws us closer to Christ.

Here's another thing to think about while we're thinking. Our emotions are closer to us than the air outside our nostrils. They are always inside us. They impact our lives in deep and profound ways, affecting our inner person and the way we feel about the world around us. Sometimes they can be very intense. We all struggle with emotions from time to time, and since they are a part of who we are, we need to learn to deal with them. They aren't going away! But that's OK. God gave them to us for a reason.

The test that we can use to decide whether or not to allow a particular emotion to run its course in our lives is to decide what the final outcome of that emotion or action will be. If the outcome is something God would condemn, put a stop to it immediately—and never go back.

BE MIND-FULL

Remember, purity isn't perfection. It's not even total victory in the here and now. Stuff happens. That's why we have to put some intentional discipline and investment into our relationships with God. We are pursuing holiness, and that requires effort, prayer, grace, and obedience. We are careful to keep our minds full of the good stuff. Our minds are soil, and it's up to us to monitor what kinds of seeds are planted in them.

In the same way a farmer doesn't just "hope" for a crop without planting seeds, you and I can't just pray and hope sinful habits will disappear. A farmer prepares the ground, plants, and cares for his crops.

Although a habit or activity might not be "sinful" according to biblical guidelines, if we allow it to dominate our lives, it can become sin to us. Our minds can be filled with distractions that displace our priorities.

Your brain is miraculous! It has the ability to remember things in incredible detail. All our sensory perceptions are absorbed into our brains where our beliefs are influenced and controlled. We live in a world where we're going to hear junky stuff. Just going to buy new socks you can hear trashy music, but what are we choosing to dwell on, to feed ourselves?

PURITY IS NOT "DOING," IT'S "BEING" THAT AFFECTS "DOING."

Some religions teach that to have a pure heart you have to perform certain things. It could be a certain devotion or carrying an object considered holy. Being pure isn't about what you do and don't do—it's about being surrendered to the Lord. Purity is about who you are in the core of your being.

It's in our minds that we make choices that affect our destinies. It can be easy to ignore what's at the end of a path when the beginning looks like fun. Please be careful not to make choices that set your feet on a path that leads you away from God's best for your life.

Have you ever chosen to do something you know you shouldn't and then asked God to keep you safe? Could we really ask Jesus to protect us all the while we are willfully making stupid choices that set us up for failure?

GOD'S MIND ON THE MATTER

"I will not let anyone walk through my mind with their dirty feet."
~ *Mahatma Gandhi*

Jesus talked in plain language about what makes a person dirty. The Pharisees were all wrapped up in the outer, ceremonial things like hand washing and counting out seeds for tithes. The Lord never said not to be careful, even in the small things, but He did correct them for not understanding or submitting to the righteousness of God (Romans 10:1-3). Jesus taught that more important than observing ceremonial laws were the evil thoughts in the hearts of men (Matthew 15:17-20). Evil thoughts bring true "defilement." Jesus specifically mentioned murder, adultery, fornication, stealing, bearing false witness, and blasphemy. That's a whole lot of bad stuff that defiles a person, and right smack dab in the middle of the list is the word "fornication."

Fornication includes all sexual activity between a male and a female who are not married to each other.

I hope as you read this book you do not get the impression that Christians should disapprove of sexuality or consider it dirty or sinful. Physical intimacy is a beautiful gift of God that the devil has attempted to deform through deception. We shouldn't be surprised that Satan manipulates and lies to us about sexuality. He's been a liar and the father of lies from the beginning of time (John 8:44). Why is he so caught up with destroying what God made to be enjoyed throughout your marriage?

Unlike fornication, marriage relationships are not just about having a good time right here and now, and the devil knows it. That's why he twists God's beautiful gifts and plans. "Surely you shall not die," he whispers; but surely, according to the Bible, those who defile themselves in this manner will not be saved (I Corinthians 6:9-10).

What kind of tricks does Satan use? He taunts a girl with threats that her boyfriend is going to drop her if she doesn't take care of his desires. I have to ask you, in all sincerity, who needs a guy like that anyway? Is this a picture of Christ giving Himself to the church? No. That's the picture of selfishness.

Another sneaky tactic is to convince people to get technical about defining sex and purity. Some say that unless you go all the way, you are still pure. It's not true. As much as I really don't want to get into the particulars, there are ways to experience intimacy that don't make babies. Genital touching of any kind is not keeping things pure. If a guy touches a girl with his private parts on any part of her body, head to toe, that's sex.

Satan also uses the lie "Everyone is doing it," often coupled with "and you are missing out." I know you've heard this before, but if some fool jumped off a bridge, would you jump, too? We can't just follow the crowd on morality issues. Use that brain God gave you!

Many girls have fallen for the lie that having an intimate relationship will fill the void in her heart. Relationships don't work that way. Sadly, this void is common among girls whose fathers are absent or uninvolved.

For girls who have unmet emotional needs from lack of a father's affection, I pray the Lord—the Comforter and "Father of the fatherless" (Psalm 68:5)—will help you fill that void. No person can make us complete, but we can be complete in Him (Colossians 2:10). The Creator of mankind made us with a void in our hearts for Jesus to fill. Everything we put there—whether it seems like a good thing at the time or an obvious bad choice—will ultimately leave us empty. And we will remain in bondage until God frees us and then provides the only true satisfaction.

Satan is an experienced liar, and he knows how to tailor the perfect lie for you. Don't listen!

When Satan tells you God is keeping you from pleasure—the same tactic he used on Eve—stop and think! Satan tricked Eve with an idea. He asked her to consider something he had to say over what God said and to decide for herself what was best.

When God says no to something, we should, too! Don't engage in conversation with the tempter. Never give up a really good thing for something that just looks good—which is Satan's inferior, corrupt plan that will leave us feeling isolated and imprisoned.

Our flesh does not want to wait, especially when it seems no one else is. It would be much easier to conform to the world we live in and give in to our desires and impulses. But, doesn't that put people, God's magnificent creations, on the same level as soulless animals like dogs and bunnies? Just doing what comes natural without thought of the consequences is an inferior way to live. God gave us our minds so we could be more than base creatures who serve our instincts over our rational understanding of what is right and wrong, pure and impure.

From birth we are led around by our carnal natures like a pig with a ring in its nose. That's natural. That's babyish. That's self-centered. It's not wrong when you're a baby, but God wants His people to be transformed! How does this happen? By renewing our minds. We are told in Romans 12:2, "Be not conformed to this world: but be ye transformed by the renewing of your mind, that ye may prove what is that good, and acceptable, and perfect, will of God."

Imagine something with me. Picture what happens inside a cell phone when it gets an update on its operating system. What happens to the old operating system? The old version gets replaced with the new, improved one. If you keep the same phone very long, you might get several upgrades. Now picture your brain getting upgraded every time you read the Bible. Some of the original programming may still be "in there," but it's being written over and enhanced all the time!

If you're careless in Bible reading, you will likely be careless in Christian living!

MIND GAMES

Guys struggle with visual temptations, while girls more often with "emotional imaginations." When we are only fantasizing about things, not acting on them, we can fool ourselves into thinking we're OK. We rationalize that our dream-world activities aren't real sexuality, but we can give so much of ourselves away in an imaginary world.

I do not want anyone to feel guilty for the occasional thought that races through their head. Everyone has them from time to time. They fly at us out of nowhere, and there's no sin in that. Sin enters our hearts when we entertain ungodly desires or fantasize about the "what-ifs." It's like the difference between a mosquito bite and a tick that latches on until you remove it.

Don't play mind games with yourself, daydreaming about what "it" might be like to be with this guy or that. If you are serious about a young man, and you find yourself falling into imaginings, train your brain to go in a positive direction—like worshiping God together.

Determine to win the battleground in your heart and mind, before entering the battleground of dating.

TIPS FOR THE TRIP

- Spend time in the Word and prayer. You can gain and regain mental and emotional strength in your mind. It's where you store truth.
- Keep your thoughts and emotions fixed, and you can live in peace (Isaiah 26:3).
- Think on the beautiful things that are true and right and lovely (Philippians 4:6-8).
- Remember that the battleground for your soul is in your mind. The devil attacks us in our heads (that's why it's important to have the helmet of salvation).

- Pray for God to cleanse and renew your mind, and to give you the right perspective as you face different situations throughout your day (Ephesians 4:23).
- Filter out lies, gossip, and trash from negative sources like celebrity "news" or pessimistic people. Don't spend time on things that bring you down by filling your mind with junk.
- Replace unhealthy or deceptive thoughts with wholesome, truth-filled Scripture.
- Purpose to be spiritually minded (Romans 8:5-6). Think about God throughout the day. If you let your thoughts wander, they can lead you astray.
- Reject ungodly imaginations and rebellious thoughts; choose to make them obedient to the Lord (II Corinthians 10:5).

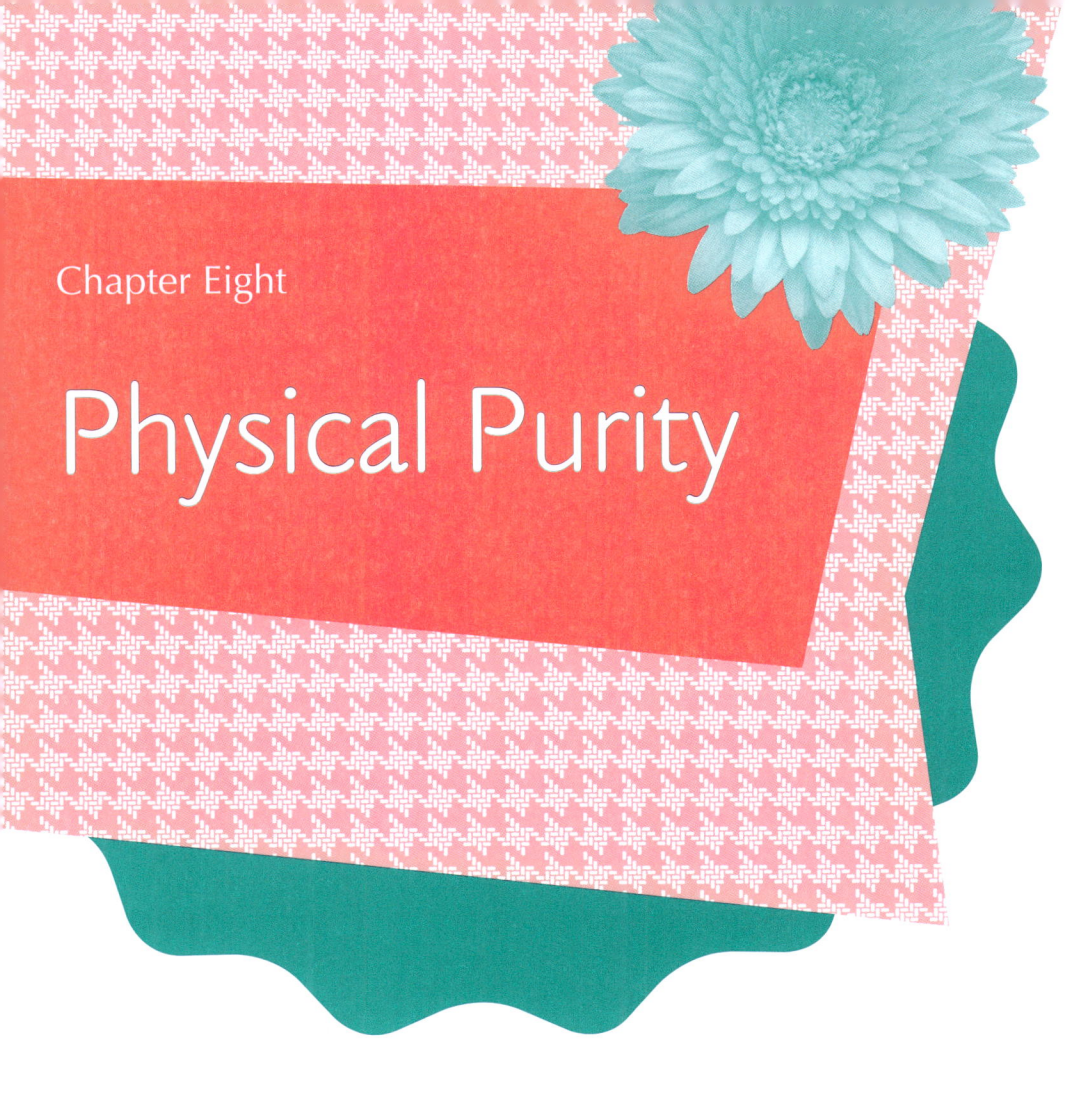

Chapter Eight

Physical Purity

Heart Soul Mind Strength

We've talked about loving the Lord with all our hearts, souls, and minds. Let's look at loving Him with all our strength. *Thayer's Greek Lexicon* gives us some insight into what it means to love God in this way. The word "strength" means force, might, and power. It specifically includes "over external things" and refers to the extent of one's ability.[11]

Loving the Lord with all your strength includes your inner strength, which has power over external things. Clearly our bodies are "external things." Souls are eternal. They live beyond the short span we spend on earth. Although our temporal bodies will not last in their present form, the Lord does have important things to say about how we handle them.

"Now may the God of peace Himself sanctify you entirely; and may your spirit and soul and body be preserved complete, without blame at the coming of our Lord Jesus Christ" (I Thessalonians 5:23, NASB). Did you see that? Each of us is supposed to be set apart and blameless—in our spirits, and souls, and bodies.

We honor God in the way we respect the bodies He gave us. This includes everything from hygiene to nutrition to cutting and drug use. We should take care of our bodies by avoiding things that damage them like alcohol and cigarettes. If a person has a pure heart, they shouldn't need these things to make them feel better. A pure heart is its own reward. It feels great! No hallucinogens or mind-altering drugs necessary! The sad result of those who get involved with these substances is that they often turn onto a path of poor decision making.

God's ultimate plan for your physical body is for it to be the place where He lives with you on this earth (I Corinthians 6:19). When God joins you, living in the temple of your body, in everything you do, He should be happy about doing them with you. That is why our conduct is important.

The Bible doesn't hold back on God's command to keep the body pure from sexual immorality: "Now the body is not for fornication, but for the Lord; and the Lord for the body" (I Corinthians 6:13). God designed sexual intimacy. It's a beautiful expression of love that creates life. Let's keep intimacy precious.

Physical intimacy is one of the earliest and most base relations between males and females. It is from this physical union that families are built. God's vision for the family—from the Garden of Eden to New Jerusalem—has always been one of purity in the husband-wife relationship.

When we think about God's plan for marriage, and the way it joins a couple together in their minds, bodies, and spirits, settling for anything less just seems like settling. Nothing compares to the beauty of marital "oneness" in a relationship and the "wholeness" experienced in the purity of that union.

> **Purity isn't about "not doing it";
> it's about saving the wonderful bond of
> intimacy for your true love.**

The "marriage bed" is a term used in the Bible to describe the place of intimacy between a man and wife. The "marriage bed" is undefiled, or pure, but outside of marriage, that's another story. One of the reasons it's so important is that what you do with your body affects your mind and spirit. You can't take your spirit or your brain out of your body to participate in intimate acts. Your eternal soul participates with you.

CHASTITY

Chastity, to some, is a rather old-fashioned word. It simply means physical purity. Abstinence means the same thing.

> **"Chastity is the most unpopular of
> the Christian virtues."**
> ~ C. S. Lewis

Why did C. S. Lewis write that chastity is the most unpopular of the Christian virtues? It could be because it's not always fun or easy. It is, however, always the right thing to do.

Purity is definitely not promoted in our society. Our American culture goes so far as to mock what God says is honorable and good. (See Jude 1:8.) The code of conduct for a Christian is often far different than what society accepts as its norm. You see, if you and I are Christians, that means we *belong* to God, even our bodies. We were bought with the price of Jesus' precious blood. Did you ever consider that if your body belongs to Him, you need His permission to join it to someone else?

In short, sexual immorality is not to be part of a Christian's life when they are single or married. Purity is for life, not just now. There are boundaries for sexuality both inside and outside marriage.

In today's world, there's a lot of "hooking up." People connect for physical pleasure without any commitment at all. They think it's perfectly fine, but there's scientific information that might surprise the "hooking up" crowd.

Neuroscientists have discovered that people record intimate experiences deep in the emotional centers of their brains. From holding hands to going all the way, your brain remembers experiences and images. The chemicals released during intimacy create a strong bond that doesn't go away just because the guy rides off into the sunset. Once two people become sexually intimate, they are a part of each other for life. The Scripture bears it out: "Do you not know that he who unites himself with a prostitute is one with her in body? For it is said, 'The two will become one flesh'" (I Corinthians 6:16, NIV). The apostle Paul was referring to a prostitute, but the concept of flesh uniting applies to anyone engaged in intimate relations.

"When you sleep with someone your body makes a promise whether you do or not." This statement was made by Lauren Winner, author of *Real Sex: The Naked Truth about Chastity*.[12]

THE "DON'T BE" ATTITUDES

Scripture gives Christians a lot of insight on the things we should be. Following are a few things we should not be engaged in:

Don't Be...

A bad "helper"

In the beginning Eve was created as a helper. There's just something in a girl that wants to help her man, but helping has its parameters, dear single girl.

It doesn't help your guy or you to do things contrary to God's Word. Sure your fella has desires, but if a girl "helps" him with these physical desires outside of God's guidelines, is she helping him to be, and become, a man of God?

Don't Be... **A rationalizer**

Don't compare yourself to others by saying things like, "At least I'm not doing that!" Sex isn't just about "going all the way." Any kind of sexual activity should be under the covering of marriage. Any sexual activity outside of marriage is sin. There. I said it, and it's an absolute truth. There's just no getting around it.

Don't Be... **A self-satisfier**

When we think "sexual intimacy" we should think "marriage," even when the topic is self-gratification. Sex is more than the act of a man and woman becoming one in a physical union. If a person is engaged in any sexual activity, that is sex.

Masturbation is a person having sex with himself, usually accompanied with thoughts of sex with another person. These thoughts can come from a person's own imagination or watching things that stimulate them. The truth is, self-gratification is a lonely and often addictive behavior. God wants us to be pure when we are alone or with others.

Don't Be...

A slave

"God paid a great price for you. So don't become slaves of anyone else" (I Corinthians 7:23, CEV). Sex can make you a slave, "imprisoning" you to others and to your own fleshly desires. There's really no such thing as "casual sex." Intimate contact always has some kind of string that attaches you to the person you are involved with.

Sex connects, and sometimes those connections take a long time to get over. It would be in your best interest to avoid the drama and wasted time it can take trying to get over something that should never have happened in the first place.

> "In forfeiting the sanctity of sex ... we forfeit something we cannot well do without. There is dullness, monotony, sheer boredom in all of life when virginity and purity are no longer protected and prized. By trying to grab fulfillment everywhere, we find it nowhere."
> ~ Elisabeth Elliott[13]

KEEP IT REAL

"How far is too far?" Dear friend, I know it's a question unmarried girls ask, but can we just be real simple and honest and say this: If you have any clothes off, you've already gone too far. Of course, it's possible to have inappropriate contact with your clothing on, but this is a really safe guideline—both people fully dressed at all times.

How is a girl to keep her mind and body pure if she continues to delve into sexual activity? If you don't start, you won't have to stop. That is the easier course to take. It's your decision. Choose wisely.

I have a scriptural answer for the question. Paul told Timothy to treat the young women in the church "as sisters, with absolute purity" (I Timothy 5:2, NIV).

KISSING AND STUFF

I'm not telling you to kiss or not to kiss (although I'm not recommending it). The truth is, some families and cultures kiss a lot! Every time you come or go you get double-cheeked smackers. Kissing can signify affection, celebration, grief, comfort, and respect. We kiss boo-boos. Some people kiss the ground when they get off an airplane!

What I do want to tell you about kissing is this: There is a difference between a kiss of greeting and romantic kissing. Romantic kissing is *designed* to lead to more. It sends triggers throughout your body and arouses passion and desires. Kissing encourages feelings of attachment and affection.

choose wisely.

When you look at what really happens in the process, kissing can be pretty gross. Saliva, bacteria, even chewed up food can be involved. Hundreds, perhaps even millions of bacterial colonies, can move from one mouth to another during a kiss.[14] There are no real "cooties," but very real diseases can be transmitted through kissing: mono, herpes, or meningitis.

Let's talk about romantic kissing and what types of sensations it can cause. Starting at the mouth, nerves carry messages from your lips, tongue, and face to your brain. Your brain is like, "woohoo!" and starts producing hormones that develop feelings of attachment and pleasure and increase the heart rate. Va-va-voom! That's why a kiss can feel so good. A hormone party goes on in the brain, blood vessels dilate, and the whole body receives more oxygen than usual.

Kissing brings people close enough to smell each other, and that brings another "connecting" sense into the play.[15] That may sound weird, but I imagine there is someone you know who has a distinct smell that brings back memories (good or bad). Perhaps your grandma wore the same perfume for fifty years. When I smell sawdust, I think of my daddy in his workshop.

There's a song that says "a kiss is just a kiss"—not true! There's chemistry involved. During a kiss, bodies naturally respond in ways that prepare them for physical intimacy. Premarital, romantic kissing is rooted in emotion and sexual desire. It stirs up passion that isn't lawful to be satisfied, according to Scripture.

Following is what I wrote on the subject of kissing in my book, *Gates & Fences: Straight Talk in a Crooked World*:

"This type of behavior is not going to enhance your relationship. It will actually make it more difficult for you to get to know each other as you really are. Instead of using your time to discover your personalities, goals, dreams and convictions, it will draw your focus to the physical, cluttering your mind and distracting you from more important aspects of your relationship."[16]

Any act that would be sexually stimulating between non-married people awakens sensations that should be sleeping. Single Christian girls who allow kissing and touching without intending to satisfy the aroused desires, are engaged in defrauding—not intending to deliver on what they seem to be offering (I Thessalonians 4:6). How can this type of conduct be considered pure?

BIBLE BASICS

In the church, we cannot tolerate sexual sin, even if it is permissible in society. Scripture is just so clear, we can't ignore it: "Now the body is not for fornication, but for the Lord" (I Corinthians 6:13). Fornication is from the Greek word, *porneia* (where we get the word *pornography*). It means all possible sexual sin.

Here are three Scripture passages to consider:

"Do you not know that wrongdoers will not inherit the kingdom of God? Do not be deceived: Neither the sexually immoral nor idolaters nor adulterers nor men who have sex with men nor thieves nor the greedy nor drunkards nor slanderers nor swindlers will inherit the kingdom of God" (I Corinthians 6:9-10, NIV).

"Put to death, therefore, whatever belongs to your earthly nature: sexual immorality, impurity, lust, evil desires and greed, which is idolatry" (Colossians 3:5, NIV).

"I beseech you therefore, brethren, by the mercies of God, that ye present your bodies a living sacrifice, holy, acceptable unto God, which is your reasonable service. And be not conformed to this world: but be ye transformed by the renewing of your mind, that ye may prove what is that good, and acceptable, and perfect, will of God" (Romans 12:1-2).

CONSEQUENCES

Think about how a "saying" becomes a "saying." It happens when the words prove to be true, time after time, year after year. What is the saying I'm building up to?

"We can choose our paths, but we can't choose our consequences."

God has given us a free will. We get to make our own choices in life. When we are young, and under our parents' authority, we don't have complete freedom to make all of our choices, but certainly enough to put us on the path of blessing—or not.

As a mom, I'll give it to you straight. There's nothing—nothing—my children could do to make me love them any less. That doesn't mean I'm always proud of every choice they make, but I love them—even on days it appears they took their brains out of their heads and put them in backwards. (This is an invisible procedure performed by every teenager at least once or twice in their growing up years.)

Here's the skinny: It is in my children's power to position themselves to receive my blessings. Obedience is irresistible. **| Kindness is a magnet. |** Responsible decisions and conduct bring out the giver in me. When I see my kids doing good, I want to do them good.

I don't know a mom who enjoys correcting her children. At the same time, it is a vital part of being a loving parent. Our heavenly Father is the most loving parent ever. He won't let us flub up over and over without attempting to correct us. Sometimes it comes gently, but sometimes not so.

"Purity is safe; impurity is risky."
~ Randy Alcorn

Premarital sex can cost more than we could ever imagine. Many times our actions bring about their own consequences. If we engage in conduct that has proven results, like making babies, it shouldn't be a surprise when a baby is conceived. It's a natural byproduct of physical intimacy. When statistics tell us the incredibly high risk of contracting a sexually transmitted disease (STD), when the warts, infections, or other symptoms come, well, there they are—our invited guests!

Statistics tell the truth about same-sex relationships. Those engaged in them have much higher risks of depression and multiple partners (which means multiplied risk of contracting diseases).

Scripture is very clear in regard to same-sex relations. Romans 1:27 in the *Amplified* version says they suffer "in their own bodies and personalities the inevitable consequences and penalty of their wrong-doing." The Bible tells us that the penalty of this type of sin is "fitting" or the "due penalty for their error" (NIV).

Did you notice the *Amplified* mentions not just their bodies, but their personalities are affected? I know there are a lot of nice people who struggle in this area, but it's nothing to play around with (no sin is). Remember this: All sexual contact outside of marriage is outside of God's plan.

What does Scripture tell us about the results of sexual immorality? A lot! First, it says "Flee fornication. Every sin that a man doeth is without the body; but he that committeth fornication sinneth against his own body" (I Corinthians 6:18).

> Sexual sin is unlike any other sin. When we engage in it, we sin against our own bodies.

No one has the choice to escape the consequences of sin. Eve chose to eat the fruit in the Garden because of what she thought she would gain. What she couldn't choose were the consequences of eating it. King David committed sexual sin with Bathsheba. He repented and was restored (II Samuel 12:13-14), but being forgiven did not take the consequence away. The child that was conceived in sin died. In our lives, too, consequences will come. Sometimes they are long and painful.

Although at times our flesh and hearts have longings, it comes down to this: pay now or pay later. Don't make a dumb choice now you may pay on for the rest of your life.

Yes, our gracious Father forgives those who turn to Him, but that does not always take away the results of our actions. The choices we make now could affect our grandchildren! I know it's easier *not* to think that far ahead, but we should. Purity, or lack of purity, could become a life-and-death issue: physical death (STDs), spiritual death, and even the death of precious relationships.

DISEASE

Before we take a quick look at some real figures on STDs and adolescent pregnancy, I just want to clarify the meaning of the word "sex." Without going into all the particulars, let me assure you that all forms of sexual contact can transmit STDs. If your cells are mingling with someone else's cells, that's all it takes in some cases.

Some may tell you a "little bit of loving" is safe, but that's not always true. Imagine your boyfriend was only involved with one other person one time. They didn't even "go all the way," but he was still exposed to every person she was with … and everyone that person was with … and every person that person was with. Picture it as you cozy up to your sweetheart—the saliva and bodily fluids of hundreds of other people right there waiting to mingle with yours. It's not pretty.

Statistics no one wants to hear:
- Approximately 18.9 million new cases of STDs occur each year.
- Forty-eight percent of new STD cases in 2000 were among fifteen- to twenty-four-year-olds.
- There are currently more than twenty-five types of STDs; some are curable, others are not.
- In 2000, approximately 822,000 pregnancies occurred among fifteen- to nineteen-year-olds.
- Seven out of ten adolescent mothers drop out of high school.[17]

I know it's easy to think, "That won't happen to me," but look at those numbers!

Today, secular teachers and advisors tell kids to practice "safe sex." The truth about the kind of "protection" they offer is that the failure rate is high—scary high. Depending on the type, 12-28 percent.[18] When protection fails, sadly a young life can be forever changed—at times even ended by a "fatal attraction."

Young people (ages 15-24) account for 50 percent of all new STDs, although they represent only 25 percent of the sexually experienced population.[19] The huge increase is most likely because they engage in riskier behavior.

Some STDs, like chlamydia, gonorrhea, syphilis, and trichomoniasis, can be treated and cured if they are diagnosed early, but they often go undetected. If they aren't treated, they can result in serious problems including chronic pelvic pain, ectopic pregnancy (which can be life-threatening), cervical cancer, and infertility.

HPV is the most common STD. HPV stands for human papillomavirus and there are more than forty types that can affect both males and females in their genital areas and in their mouths and throats. Skin to skin contact is all that is required to contract HPV, and it can cause serious health problems, including genital warts and cancer. HPV can go away without treatment, but most people infected with it don't even know they have it.

Speaking of treatments, on a side note, the annual direct medical costs to treat STDs is nearly $16 billion.[20]

OTHER CONSEQUENCES

STDs are the frightening and frequent results of sexual activity, as well as out-of-wedlock pregnancies. In addition to these harsh physical consequences, let's look at some other byproducts.

DISSATISFACTION

Living a promiscuous, "free sex" lifestyle will likely take you down one of two paths: boredom or "deviant/perverse" behavior. Our society may exalt sexual activity, but does it truly satisfy? The truth is that sexually active kids are most often the ones who seem the most unfulfilled. That makes no sense, does it? Aren't they the ones having all the "fun"? There is pleasure in sin for a season, but it does not satisfy. None of the temporary things of this world will keep us happy for long. When we live for pleasure, we are never truly satisfied. When we live for the Pleasure Giver, we can be truly fulfilled.

> "By trying to grab fulfillment everywhere, we find it nowhere."
> ~ Elisabeth Eliott

GREATER RISK OF UNFAITHFULNESS

This is my theory, but I believe it is sound. Those who do not honor God's Word on sexual purity before marriage have little assurance their boyfriends, turned fiancés, turned husbands will honor God's Word on keeping their marriage bed sacred. Don't you think it's best to build a marriage on the most solid foundation possible?

VALUES DETERIORATE

When a society not only accepts but promotes sex between unmarried people, precious values like faithfulness, commitment, and loyalty are undermined and even eliminated.

OTHER PEOPLE ARE AFFECTED

There's a story in the Bible about a girl named Dinah. She was Jacob's daughter, raised to live "separate" and "holy." When the family moved, she "went out to see the daughters of the land" (Genesis 34:1). It seems she wanted to check out how the non-Jewish girls lived.

As she was experiencing life among the pagans, a prince took such a fancy to her that he took her to his tent and violated her.

I have to give some credit to the prince. It's important who you hang out with. The prince tried to make things right but in the end, there was a great loss of life and Dinah's family had to leave their new home.

Dinah might have thought she was just going to have a little fun, do a little exploring, but her choice put her on a terrible path. The consequences of her actions were much greater than her curiosity and any behaviors she might have engaged in, but this is a strong warning we should give some consideration.

Small steps away from God and His ways can cause great falls. We can't really see inside Dinah's heart, but let us be careful not to long for the lifestyles of the "pagan girls" of our days. It appears to be the beginning of her downfall, and that downfall affected all her loved ones.

MOST GUYS WANT A PURE WIFE

Don't you hate a double standard? The truth is that most guys who are sexually active before marriage don't want to marry a girl who has "been around." They want a pure girl for a wife—for the mother of their children. Is that fair? No. Is it true? For the most part.

WOUNDED RELATIONSHIPS

Many people who had sex before marriage have discovered that it did not help their relationships. What they thought would unite actually separated them as each carried their own isolating guilt. It added tension and confusion and put a wrong focus on the physical side of things. It can lead to bad marriages or bad break-ups.

BAGGAGE

If you marry someone who wasn't your first love, that can cause its own problems. I call it "baggage." When you finally

settle down and marry "the" love of your life, you don't want memories flooding your mind of experiences you had with another guy—right while you are sharing intimacy with your husband. Sex is not just a physical experience. Your heart and your mind are definitely engaged. You bring to your marriage bed all the relationships you had before.

One young man explained it this way: When you are immoral with several people, you give a piece of your heart away to each person. Then when you meet the one God intends for you to marry, you don't have your whole heart to give to that person.

BAD COPING TOOLS

Drowning pain with promiscuous behavior may bring temporary relief, but the issues remain and the behaviors make new problems. Other coping tools like substance abuse or cutting have the same bad results.

Abortion is never the right choice. For many the act of having a baby aborted haunts them the rest of their life.

> **No matter what you've done,
> don't withdraw from God.
> He's your hope and your answer!**

BROKEN HEART

I'm not saying premarital sex causes actual heart disease, but did you know it's really possible to have Broken Heart Syndrome? When a heart is healthy, there are four chambers that beat in rhythm. It's my prayer that as every chamber of our physical hearts beat in sync, our spiritual hearts pump in rhythm with God's heart!

REALITY CHECK

Not everyone will regret having sex outside of marriage, but if you're walking with the Lord, you should. It should grieve the Holy Spirit living inside you.

The conclusion of the matter is this: Sexual sin, like no other sin, can hurt you in every way: physically, emotionally, mentally, and spiritually—even financially!

John Lennon wrote a song called "Imagine." I'd like you to consider a mix of lyrics—his and mine:

Imagine there's a heaven
It's easy if you try
A real hell below us
Glory in the sky
Imagine all the people
Living for eternity …

Imagine there's no herpes
No broken hearts for me or you
No STDS to die for
AIDs or infertility, too
Imagine all the people
Living in covenant and in peace ...

You may say I'm a dreamer
But I'm not the only one
I hope someday you'll join us
And the world will be as one.

Imagine no unfaithfulness
No pornography in the land
No unplanned pregnancy
Or abortion on demand
Imagine all the people
Living in harmony ...

You may say I'm a dreamer
But I'm not the only one
This is the plan of Jesus
That the world will live as one.

Chapter Nine

Purity Plans

Sometimes life comes along and smacks us with unexpected temptations and challenges. To overcome them, we need to be prepared in advance. Getting close to God first, before getting close to anyone else, is your best strategy for keeping pure. It's been said the best defense is a good offense. You may be surprised to know that some of the worst attacks can come after a time of spiritual victory. Stay alert.

Too many Christians are not willing to make the sacrifice to serve the Lord with their whole heart. By their actions they say, "Don't ask me to serve God—I'm too busy serving myself!" As long as we serve according to the will of God, we have all the power of the throne supporting us.

Right now is the best time for you to make a firm commitment to purity!

PLAN YOUR MAN

Wouldn't it be awesome if you could go to a husband dealership like a car dealership and order exactly what you wanted? That's not reality, but it is possible to "plan your man" by deciding in advance what characteristics and qualities are important to you. You might have a certain preference about appearance, but let me say, the Lord might surprise you. It's possible to fall in love with a man who isn't anything like the kind of guy you are usually attracted to.

Before you think I'm crazy (if you don't already), I'm not talking about an order form you pray to God to fill, but it would be helpful to have a clear picture of what is important to you. If you don't intend to marry someone, you really have no reason to date them.

Envision your future with a godly husband who waited for you! If you know the character of the person you want to marry, it will help you make good choices about the kind of person to date.

> **Run as fast as you can towards God, and if someone keeps up, introduce yourself.**

Let's look at what you might want to consider "dateable" criteria, which should mean the same thing as "marriageable" criteria.

1. *A Christian*! Reserve your heart and your dates for someone who believes what you believe about God. Your husband will be the leader of your home. If you are in disagreement about your beliefs, you are setting yourself up for a life of arguments, misery, or even backsliding. That's not what God intended for marriage! Be sure of what you stand for and careful what you fall for!

2. Being a Christian is just the starting point. You want someone who does more than come to church on Sunday. Envision yourself with a person who will lead and inspire you to do more and be more. Can you see yourself being comfortable praying together, reading the Bible together, being involved in service together? Only give your heart to someone who has a passionate love for God.

3. Your would-be-babe should have similar views on the important things of day-to-day life: working, saving, giving, morality. If you are a saver, would you want to marry someone who lived on credit? If you don't want children but Mr. Wonderful wants a van-load, there may be a problem.

4. Do you have similar callings? If you were called to the mission field but your love interest had no burden for missions work, how could you fulfill the call of God in your life? Discuss those things before saying, "I do."

5. Once married, you will be talking to your husband the rest of your life. Ask yourself if you enjoy conversation as much as you'd enjoy some smooching. Once married, how much time are you going to spend talking vs. kissing and other stuff? Talking when single will keep you focused on things that aren't physical and will help you keep things pure in your relationship.

6. Only consider a relationship with a guy who is pure while single. If he won't control himself now, how can you trust him to be faithful in marriage?

7. Pray for your future husband—even if you haven't met him yet. Pray the Lord will help him grow spiritually, keep him from falling into temptation, and protect him. Praying for your future husband now will help you to conduct yourself righteously when the Lord brings you together.

These are some good starting points to build a vision of the man you want to marry. You may not marry the first guy you date. You will honor your future husband on all your dates if you keep in mind you are also honoring God. The evidence of Christian maturity is not just in what we know, but how our lives and words speak to others. When we allow God complete control in our lives, we become mature in Him.

SELF CHECK

While listing what is important to you, have you considered if your character and spirituality would meet someone else's desire for a godly wife? It's important to develop yourself and become a person someone else would be blessed to marry.

Be careful about flirting. Ask yourself, "If this guy was married, would I be talking and acting the same way around him?" If you were a married woman, would you talk to guys the same way you do now? Flirting is like a thermometer used to measure "temperature." Flirting is calculated to lead somewhere.

PLAN TO SUCCEED

It is in your best interest, young person, to mingle with people from all generations. We older folks aren't that bad. Some of us are kind of fun! If you want wisdom, you need to spend time with wise people (Proverbs

13:20). Wisdom listens to the voices of the ones who have already walked down the road.

Speaking of hanging out with the older generation, in the not-so-distant past, unmarried girls and boys were chaperoned. When they did spend time together (with an adult around), it was for the purpose of determining if they might be suitable for marriage. There wasn't a lot of emotional intimacy before the wedding. That's not saying there wasn't attraction and relationship, but emotional and physical purity are much better protected when adults are in view.

Each of us is called to guard our own heart. At the same time, we should be thankful for the people the Lord has placed in our lives to help us. Parents, youth leaders, counselors, and pastors have your best interest at heart and have invested themselves in your success. Your leaders have seen a lot more than you have. Trust them.

Don't resent your parents' desire to help you with "pre-date" interviews or guidelines. Inviting your mom and dad into your love life is a great way to keep things pure. Remember, they probably know you better than you know yourself. They have wisdom, insight, and experience and they love you! If you're afraid your dad will say no guy is right for you, well, you'll just have to trust the Lord with that fear. Choose to honor your parents; it will bring great blessing!

It's a fact that girls who are close with their fathers are less likely to fall into sexual sin. Sometimes dads pull away from showing affection to their girls once they start to develop. That can be hard. If this has happened in your family, I hope you will prayerfully talk to your dad and find mutually comfortable ways of connecting. Maybe you shouldn't be sitting on his lap anymore, but a kiss on the cheek or a side-armed hug might be good for both of you!

Believe me, your dad does not want you turning to Mr. Joe Cool in school to fill your need for affection and affirmation. Try to work through any awkwardness that may have arisen as you developed from his baby girl to his lovely daughter.

If you don't have a father figure in your life to give you the affection and affirmation you need, I'm so sorry. I wish I could wish one into your life. I can't, but the Lord has promised to be a father to the fatherless (Psalm 68:5-6). **Statistics may be against you, but with God on your side, you can be an incredible beat-the-odds success!**

Learn from your mother's wisdom and experience. She might not have grown up in church; that means she knows some things that could help you. If she did grow up in church, she knows some things that could help you. Nobody has all the answers, and yours is a personal walk, but the voice of your mother's experience could be just what you need to hear.

Be honest with your mom. Yes, even if things have gone too far, it would be best to share that with her. She can help you from falling again, and I do believe and pray she will be your biggest cheerleader.

Prepare and prevent instead of repair and repent.

SETTING BOUNDARIES

Everyone needs boundaries. You may have a curfew or guidelines set by your parents for being in cars or alone with boys. Don't resent their input; be thankful they care! While you are being thankful, be "think-full" about your personal guidelines. Some boundaries are set by parents, but you need your own deal-breaker boundary lines.

- First things first: Say "yes" to saying "no!" Decide in advance that you are waiting and worth waiting for.
- Don't allow yourself to get into compromising situations. Decide you are going to be disciplined about where you go and who you go with. I made up my own definition for "discipline." Discipline = "dis is de plan!" Make a plan and stick with it, then you will have an answer when the invitation comes. "I'm sorry. I can't do that. I have something else planned!"
- Make a firm written commitment to yourself to remain sexually pure until your wedding night. If you are in a relationship, write one out together. Set the boundary lines in the cool of the day, not the heat of the night.
- Determine now how you will stop things if you get into a tempting situation. What would you do or say if someone

touched you inappropriately? It could be as simple as "Excuse me," and then really excusing yourself—as in vamoose, get out of there, and now. A person intentionally touching you in a way they shouldn't knows what they are doing, so know what you are doing. Don't let things get out of control by being in control from the beginning.
- Stay in the light. I know it can be fun to do things at night with your friends, but sometimes, it's just not wise. When it's dark it's easier to let your guard down. Be careful.
- If you should kiss and it's more than a quick greeting or goodbye—if it turns into something prolonged or passionate—jump up and jump back right then and there. There's no 1-2-3 count. If the kiss is longer than 1, you better get out of there.
- Be honest with yourself. If you are feeling tempted, talk to God about it, not your boyfriend or your girlfriends. Ask the Lord to help you. God doesn't do the obeying for you, but He will help you obey. Don't ignore His council.

> **"Purity is the gatekeeper for everything precious and blissful in God's kingdom."**
> ~ Eric Ludy

When you make sure to have a plan, you can enjoy the sweetness of a relationship without the fear of going too far. If you ever give yourself away completely, you will never get all of yourself back. Hold on!

The best plan you can make is to chase after God. Be enthusiastic about your walk with Jesus! Enjoy it, and keep your priorities straight. The pursuit of a love relationship should never take priority over pursuing God and His will in your life.

Those who begin dating when they are young greatly increase their risk of becoming sexually active. Be patient. Lauren Barlow of the group Barlow Girl, said, "God didn't create one Adam and five Eves and say, 'Go ahead, date around and see which one you like the best.' He said, 'Adam, I know what you need and I'm going to create that for you.'" Trust God's guidance—not just for the right guy, but the right timing.

> **"In your patience possess ye your souls" (Luke 21:19).**

TEMPTATION AND TESTING

I love God. I love living for God. But if we're going to be real, we need to learn how to cope with the reality that temptations are a part of life.

To be an overcomer means a person has faced some obstacles, trials, and temptations and come out on top! God never said we wouldn't have troubles or temptations. Actually, He said we would. Our goal? To be an overcomer, not to be overcome.

The key to successfully dealing with temptation is to recognize that we can't do it alone. We need God's strength to deal with all the issues that hide deep in our hearts.

SCRIPTURAL STRATEGIES

When you're sailing stormy seas, you have a resource to turn to. The Word of God is a lifeboat. Step into it, and you will be safe. The following verses of Scripture will help you as you navigate temptations' tides.

"But each person is tempted when they are dragged away by their own evil desire and enticed. Then, after desire has conceived, it gives birth to sin; and sin, when it is full-grown, gives birth to death" (James 1:14-15, NIV).

To avoid sin being "birthed" in our lives, "conception" needs to be nipped in the bud. Don't dwell on temptations, or they will give birth to sinful actions. Jesus breaks the chains of sin. All people have broken God's law and consequently live apart from Him (Romans 3:23). But Christ's death and resurrection free us when we accept His gift of forgiveness and place our trust in Him. Then we can have a relationship with the Lord.

"Flee also youthful lusts: but follow righteousness, faith, charity, peace, with them that call on the Lord out of a pure heart" (II Timothy 2:22).

You might find it helpful to make a list of the people, places, and things that trigger impure thoughts and then do what you can to avoid them. For

example, keep spiritually strong people in the mix when you have to be around people who have caused you to stumble in the past. When it comes to things like cell phones and computers, you may want to have someone you trust install filtering software.

> **"Dearly beloved, I beseech you as strangers and pilgrims, abstain from fleshly lusts, which war against the soul" (I Peter 2:11).**

When it comes to purity, lust is the root of the problem. To be frank, lust is not just a guy problem, a girl problem, or even a single's problem—it comes with being human. Lust comes from envy and desiring things that are not good for you spiritually. That's why we need to deny the lure of worldly pleasures, knowing that we are in a war for our souls. Our carnal, or physical, person and our spiritual person will always be at odds with each other, but stay in the fight! Don't let a desire or craving become an addiction. If our flesh wins, we lose both the flesh and spirit man. In order for our spirit man to win, our fleshly longings must give way.

"Having therefore these promises, dearly beloved, let us cleanse ourselves from all filthiness of the flesh and spirit, perfecting holiness in the fear of God" (II Corinthians 7:1).

You and I are called to be actively involved in the purity process. Because we are so blessed by God and His incredible promises, we choose to live a life of purity and then dedicate ourselves to continue walking in that decision. Our life can be one of many privileges, but we must remember that our works should glorify God.

"If thy right eye offend thee, pluck it out, and cast it from thee: for it is profitable for thee that one of thy members should perish, and not that thy whole body should be cast into hell" (Matthew 5:29).

If you are continually tempted by something or someone in your life, if at all possible, cut it out. Pitch it! Ditch it! Block it! Skip it! Unfriend it! Nothing is worth eternity in Hell! Have the courage to let go of the things that are not worth holding on to.

> **"There hath no temptation taken you but such as is common to man: but God is faithful, who will not suffer you to be tempted above that ye are able; but will with the temptation also make a way to escape, that ye may be able to bear it" (I Corinthians 10:13).**

This verse has helped me through many difficult times. It is saying that you are not going to experience a temptation that others haven't experienced as well. But God is faithful, and He won't allow you to be tempted beyond your ability to withstand the temptation. No, it's quite the contrary. He will make a way of escape. He liberates us from persistent sins like jealousy, bitterness, and gluttony. His Spirit resides within each believer and provides the power to overcome wrong choices that seemed to "own" us. He enables us to do what He desires—by bringing immediate healing or by giving guidance and strength in the ongoing battle.

> **"Finally, my brethren, be strong in the Lord, and in the power of his might. Put on the whole armour of God, that ye may be able to stand against the wiles of the devil" (Ephesians 6:10-11).**

I didn't take the time to list all the armor here, but I recommend going to Ephesians 6 and learning just what you can put on to protect your head, your heart, your feet, and even your loins! Get in the Word. There you will find all the tools you need to truly overcome whatever comes your way.

"Confess your faults one to another, and pray one for another, that ye may be healed. The effectual fervent prayer of a righteous man availeth much" (James 5:16).

If you are struggling, be honest with yourself and a trusted Christian friend. Tell someone who loves you what you are dealing with. Pray for each other. What a difference that could make in a youth group! Imagine a group of young people holding each other accountable, praying for one another, celebrating their victories together. I would love to see that!

I see kids posting things online about "forever friends," and I just have to say that a forever friend is interested in your forever. A true friend should be concerned with helping you develop your character and prepare for your future (Proverbs 27:17).

"Be not deceived: evil communications corrupt good manners" (I Corinthians 15:33).

If we keep bad company, it will corrupt our good character. One bad spirit can poison another. Spirits are contagious! Be cautious and reserve your closest relationships for people who are spiritually strong.

There may be a wrong way to do the right thing, but there's never a right way to do the wrong thing.

MOUNTAINOUS MOLEHILLS

How do you make a mountain out of molehill? Add more dirt. If you keep throwing dirt on a little mound, it will get bigger and bigger.

When we continue to walk away from a temptation, the pull of our passions lessen and we draw closer to God. When you mess up in your thoughts (and we all do), immediately go to the Lord in repentance. Ask Him to forgive you and help you get it right.

One verse that has encouraged me for years is Habakkuk 3:19. Let's look at it in the *Amplified* version:

"The Lord God is my Strength, my personal bravery, and my invincible army; He makes my feet like hinds' feet and will make me to walk [not to stand still in terror, but to walk] and make [spiritual] progress upon my high places [of trouble, suffering, or responsibility]!"

If you are serious about doing the will of God, you have to burn the bridge that takes you back to the world.

> **It's not our weaknesses that get us, it's our weak moments."**
> ~ Raymond Woodward

YOUR TEACHER

Our minds must be disciplined to the Word of God. That's the reason we are told in Colossians 3:16 to "let the word of Christ dwell in you richly in all wisdom." A covenant relationship with God is a partnership, a loving working relationship. It might feel like life would be so much easier following the ways of the world. It might even seem impossible to do things God's way. If it was, God would not have asked it of us. The Lord has given us a teacher to help along the way.

"For the grace of God that bringeth salvation hath appeared to all men, teaching us that, denying ungodliness and worldly lusts, we should live soberly, righteously, and godly, in this present world" (Titus 2:11-12).

Our teacher's name is "Grace." Some wrongly believe that grace excuses sin, but that is far from true. God's grace trains us to reject ungodliness and inappropriate, lustful desires. It teaches us to live self-controlled, upright, and godly lives. Ask the Lord to teach you how through His beautiful instructor—His grace that gives us the strength we need to live a godly life. *Grace* is defined as "undeserved love and unmerited favor." We did nothing to deserve the kind of love Christ has bestowed on us, but His mercy has provided a promise of abundant life.

Grace doesn't say, "Anything goes!" Grace says, "Unrighteousness has to go!"

Daily put yourself in God's hands, spend time in His presence, and ask Him to show you how to live pleasing to Him. Ask the Lord to transform your desires according to His Word and by His

grace. Listen to the words of I Peter 1:13-16: "Wherefore gird up the loins of your mind, be sober, and hope to the end for the grace that is to be brought unto you at the revelation of Jesus Christ; as obedient children, not fashioning yourselves according to the former lusts in your ignorance: but as he which hath called you is holy, so be ye holy in all manner of conversation; because it is written, Be ye holy; for I am holy."

Find a mentor or teacher in your life. This can be anyone who loves the Lord. The older and wiser teach the younger, or those who are ignorant of the truth. Many things are learned through experience—so learn from the experienced. Every word of God can be applied to our lives in some way.

TESTING

Testing is different from temptation. The Lord allows us to be tested for several reasons. One is so that we can know where we need to grow. Another is so that by coming through each test we become stronger. Remember the story in Genesis of Abraham actually planning to sacrifice Isaac? The angel of the Lord stopped him at the last moment and God said, "Now I know" that you fear me. Abraham passed the test. He was willing to obey God at any cost. When we pass each test that comes to us then God will "know" that we love Him above any test that comes our way.

> **"He shall sit as a refiner and purifier of silver: and he shall purify the sons of Levi, and purge them as gold and silver, that they may offer unto the Lord an offering in righteousness" (Malachi 3:3).**

The Lord wants you to know what's inside that needs to be cleansed so you can walk in righteousness with Him. While you're going through testing, remember to hang on to God. He has good plans for your life (Jeremiah 29:11).

"Howbeit when he, the Spirit of truth, is come, he will guide you into all truth" (John 16:13). God will never ask you to do anything He will not empower you to do. Remember this: He is not speaking to your fleshly nature but to your Spirit-filled nature, and He knows what He is capable of doing for His glory if you will allow it.

LORI'S LIST

In addition to all the wonderful verses of Scripture, here are a few recommendations that may help you handle temptation.

- Journal. Writing things down can help you release some of the pressure and deal with things rationally.

- When you are in a relationship, remember these two cardinal rules:
    1. Stay public. Always stay in a safe, well-lit environment with other people around.
    2. Stay vertical. Never, never, never lie down together. That's what husbands and wives do.
- Remember, just because a boy expects something doesn't mean you should do it. Don't allow someone else's convictions to determine your boundary lines.
- Don't spend time with a boyfriend until you've spent some time with God.
- Pay attention to the red flags in any relationship, such as mocking, disobedience, or impure conversations. That "red flag" is the Holy Ghost giving you discernment.
- Keep your heart and head going in the right direction and your feet will take care of themselves.

Be aware that purity is attractive, and not just to the pure at heart. Some less-than-pure people consider it a conquest to claim another's innocence.

Get on fire for God! If you are burning with godly passion, you will be too hot for Satan to handle and temptation will not be able to take hold.

Chapter Ten

Waiting
(It's Worth It!)

Several years ago I had the opportunity to talk with a young lady whose heart was fluttering on the wings of romance. She was young. It was her first kind-of boyfriend-ish relationship. His name was Eric. He was a guy from school. He was *soooo* cute.

As we drove down the road, talking about him and how relationships can develop into more than we anticipate if we aren't careful, I remembered her love for potato chips.

"You know how you think you can open a bag of chips and eat just one?" I asked her.

"Yeah," she said.

"Well, it's like that with boys. You want to have just one kiss. You think you'll be happy with one, but that kiss is so sweet and exciting you think you will have just one more. The kisses keep coming, and before you know it, you've eaten the whole bag."

The girl smiled—and I knew she got the picture.

"You know what I'm going to call Eric from now on?" I asked. "I'm going to call him Chip. Whenever I see you, I'm going to ask how Chip is doing."

She laughed, and over the next few weeks I asked her about Chip. It wasn't long before the "puppy love" passed.

I hoped my young friend was glad she hadn't opened the "bag of chips" and prayed she would remember this example the next time a tempting package came along.

"Young men do not respect girls they can take advantage of—and they do not as easily take advantage of girls they respect."
~ Sarah Mally

GOOD AND PERFECT

"Every good gift and every perfect gift is from above, and cometh down from the Father of lights, with whom is no variableness, neither shadow of turning" (James 1:17). When it comes to good, perfect, and excellent gifts, they all have one thing in common. They come from God. He's the source, and not only is He the giver of the good, perfect gifts, His bright character never changes.

It's interesting that this verse comes right after James' warning to be careful about being tempted and lured away by our own cravings. Everyone has cravings, but if we allow them to conceive, they give birth to sin. When sin grows up, it gives birth to death (James 1:15).

If you struggle with the fear of being alone in life, remember the words in I John 4:18: "Perfect love casteth out fear." Let the perfect love of God, resting and trusting in His good plans for your life, push the fear far from you. (Read Jeremiah 29:11.)

I want to encourage you today, beautiful daughter of the Most High God. There are guys out there looking for a girl just like you—who is waiting for a guy just like them.

TESTIMONY

HER STORY: *I walked down the aisle in my white wedding gown, excited to become one with my life mate. It was pure joy to know that I was giving all of myself to him. My life, my love, and my body was preserved solely for him.*

With God's help, we saved ourselves for only each other and the covenant we were making to each other and God. Sexual purity allowed for a foundation of trust and confidence.

God's way is always the best. Purity before marriage builds compounding interest leading to the wealth of a godly marriage.

Walking down the aisle in white may only be a tradition to some, but for me it was an outward representation of an inward purity of spirit, soul, and body preserved for my husband.

~ Lindsi Walker

HIS STORY: *There is an eloquent verse in the Bible I pray often. James 1:17 says, "Every good gift and every perfect gift is from above."*

The gift of purity is indeed a good and perfect gift. The confusion of our culture depicts moral purity as restrictive, archaic, and regulatory. However, the truth of God's timeless Word rings true in Galatians 5:1. God's plan of purity provides the ultimate life of liberty. Immorality enacts fleeting pleasure with the enduring yoke of bondage.

The compelling attraction I had to Lindsi was beyond her outward beauty. She had a pure body and spirit. Purity is a priceless treasure. Her inward beauty radiated with the virtues of Christ. Giving myself away to Lindsi with the mutual gift of purity was a godly cornerstone in building a lasting marital covenant.

~ Jonathan Walker

PURITY PROSPERS

Psalm 1 is one of the most beautiful passages in Scripture. Not only is it poetic, it gives important information on just what happens to the godly and the ungodly. Verse 3 says, "He shall be like a tree planted by the rivers of water, that bringeth forth his fruit in his season; his leaf also shall not wither; and whatsoever he doeth shall prosper."

"Be like a tree" is a slogan of sorts. When I think of it, I think about the blessings promised to the godly person. I want those blessings, don't you? Who wouldn't want to be strong, fruitful, life-giving, and prosperous?

The beatitudes are another great source of inspiration (Matthew 5). They tell us both what to "be" and the right "attitudes" we should have (get it, the be-attitudes?). When we have the right actions and attitudes, God's blessings are promised to follow.

In all our daily choices, we either "sow to the flesh" or "sow to the Spirit" (Galatians 6:8). With our actions and thoughts, we plant seeds that affect what kind of person we're growing into and the level of impact our lives will have for God. "The flesh" is the part of us that wants to live and act independently of the Lord. As humans, all of us have to deal with the pull of this attitude; we don't lose it automatically when we're saved. However, the Holy Ghost frees us from slavery to the flesh. God begins to change us so we can turn from the lure of living for self and instead start to live according to the truth. The choices we make contribute to helping us mature spiritually.

REWARD

There's a little phrase I've been using lately: "tracking with God." Picture Jesus laying down one rail and you laying another right beside it—creating a track of sorts like for a railroad or roller coaster. It's a visual for me of choosing to go where God is going, running along the same path.

The psalmist wrote "I will run the way of thy commandments, when thou shalt enlarge my heart" (Psalm 119:32). God's commandments will never take us in the wrong direction. When we walk alongside the Lord, we will experience Him in greater ways, live in His presence, bear fruit, and bring Him glory.

Sometimes "tracking with Jesus" may lead us into a tight place or narrow way, but the narrow road is the one that leads to life (Matthew 7:13-14). One really awesome thing I love about Jesus is that He doesn't just lead us in the way; Jesus *is* the way, and He is our reward for walking in the way (Genesis 15:1).

What could be more important than having Jesus for our reward? Nothing! Paul counted all things as loss; he gave everything to know and follow Jesus. What are we willing to give?

> "You have made us for yourself, and our heart is restless until it rests in you." [21]
> ~ Augustine

Walking the pure path brings peace.

BLESSED CHURCHES

One thing I know for certain that helps to establish a person in their walk with God is involvement. Those who are introduced to ministry at a young age learn the fulfillment of being busy in the kingdom of God. They learn how to strengthen and bless others. They are privileged to witness firsthand the wonders and workings of the Holy Ghost. They begin to grow in their knowledge of the ways of God and begin to take "ownership" of the church.

| **Being pure blesses your church!** | This is true on many levels. First, to put it simply, blessed people bring blessings to their churches.

Another aspect is less drama and discord. Truth be told, "stuff" will come out at one time or another and can cause hurts and side-taking that is not healthy in the house of God. Being pure in your heart, mind, spirit, and strength promotes peace and unity in your local church.

TO FEAR, OR NOT TO FEAR

Not only are there blessings to gain, there is a Hell to shun. We need to remember that! There's nothing wrong with a healthy dose of the fear of the Lord every now and again to keep us on the right path. "The fear of the Lord is the beginning of wisdom: a good understanding have all they that do his commandments" (Psalm 111:10). This does not mean that we are afraid of

God but that we stand in awe of Him for "great is the LORD, and greatly to be praised; and his greatness is unsearchable" (Psalm 145:3).

> **"The fear of the Lord shouldn't scare us out of our wits; it should scare us *into* them."**
> *~ Randy Alcorn*

Although fear isn't a great long-term motivator, realizing there are negative consequences can help us make right choices. While we are on the subject, sometimes fear can lead us to make poor choices, as well. Look at this powerful verse in II Timothy 1:7: "For God hath not given us the spirit of fear; but of power, and of love, and of a sound mind." We have nothing to fear when we become a born again child of God.

Be very sensitive to the Spirit of God. We can never do the work of God without a relationship with Him. What could happen if we all truly fell in love with Jesus? There is power in His presence, and love is stronger than fear! Are you one of those people who appear happy and seem to have life figured out, yet inside feel uneasy, fearful, and empty? Jesus Christ is the only One who can redeem you, forgive your sins, and fill the vacant place in your soul. Allow Him to liberate you today.

There are many ways you can learn to yield to the Spirit and not to your own understanding. Take time to read the following verses of Scripture which will help you to overcome life's temptations.

Eyes yielded – Hebrews 12:2
Tongue yielded – Ephesians 4:21-25
Hands yielded – Ecclesiastes 9:10
Heart yielded – Psalm 51:10
Ears yielded – Acts 8:26
Feet yielded – Ephesians 6:15

Be "as obedient children, not fashioning yourselves according to the former lusts in your ignorance: but as he which hath called you is holy, so be ye holy in all manner of conversation" (I Peter 1:14-15).

Chapter Eleven

Restoration

Sometimes our most bitter lessons are the sweetest to know. If you have fallen in the area of purity, I have something to tell you. Jesus paid to redeem you—all of you—your whole heart, soul, mind, and body. Think about this: What pit could you fall into that Jesus couldn't lift you from? Once He has brought us out, just looking back to what we were before will be incentive and inspiration enough to keep us moving forward, ever closer to Him, Christ our Savior!

If you fall, don't be like Adam and Eve and try to hide from God (like He didn't know where they were—yeah, right). King David messed up, and he is called a man after God's own heart! If someone like David, who had a pure heart with God, can make a mistake and be restored, so can you. What was his prayer?

"Create in me a clean heart, O God; and renew a right spirit within me. Cast me not away from thy presence; and take not thy holy spirit from me. Restore unto me the joy of thy salvation; and uphold me with thy free spirit" (Psalm 51:10-12).

STARTING

David acknowledged his sin, asked the Lord's forgiveness, and then prayed for cleansing, renewal, and a return of the joy of his salvation. When a Christian falls into sin, they lose their spiritual joy, and the joy of the Lord is what gives us strength

(Nehemiah 8:10). Strength, joy, and salvation are one of God's sweet package deals (Psalm 118:14).

I don't believe the Lord is mad at a person who makes mistakes. The truth is, God is mad *about* you! Christian author Max Lucado expressed it this way: "If God had a refrigerator, your picture would be on it. If He had a wallet, your photo would be in it." God hates sin, not sinners. Why does He despise sin so much? I believe at least one reason is because sin separates us from Him. He wants to be in a pure and holy relationship with His children, and sin gets in the way.

| **God's goal, however, is your success.** | If you've fallen, believe that it is His heartfelt desire for you to get up, get right, and get going! Don't be discouraged. You can do this.

Discouragement is faith in the devil. Have faith in God!

You may have been disobedient, but you will not be defeated if you get back up again!

Apostle Paul said, "We have this treasure in earthen vessels, that the excellency of the power may be of God, and not of us. We are troubled on every side, yet not distressed; we are perplexed, but not in despair; persecuted, but not forsaken; cast down, but not destroyed" (II Corinthians 4:7-9).

Don't doubt God's devotion, and don't focus on obstacles. Faith sees the way, and Jesus is the way! Obstacles are those awful things we see when we take our eyes off the goal.

God told Cain if he would do right he would be blessed, but if he chose wrong, sin crouched at the door (Genesis 4:7). Cain was given the opportunity to do right.

When Jesus talked with the woman caught in adultery, He told her, "Go and sin no more." He offered her forgiveness and a chance to get things right. If you used to serve sin, you can be made free from it and serve righteousness instead.

"For a healthy heart, exercise your faith!"
~ Lynette O'Donnell

PURE FREEDOM

Jesus Christ has the power to free you from any and all addictions or bondage—from pornography to the physical stuff. We all need Jesus. Not one person is sinless. One of the most encouraging verses in the Bible, in my opinion, is the one that says, "and such were some of you" (I Corinthians 6:11). There were people involved in all kinds of mess, including sexual sin, that were freed from their pasts. What they were, they were not anymore!

There is power available to those who trust in Jesus! Lean on His strength, trust in His grace, and then take the steps you need to see things change in your life. God's grace makes it possible for you and me to be free from immorality at every level. True liberty is found in the goodness and grace of God Who nailed our sins to His cross (Colossians 2:13-14).

God's got this if you will let Him and work with Him. Track with Jesus! He not only wants to forgive sinners, but also cleanse them from the junky, worthless feelings that sin leaves in their lives. It's up to the individual to choose to surrender their shame to the One who came to give them victory. Freedom is a choice, and it comes when we choose to discipline ourselves, listen to our teacher named Grace, and walk with the Spirit of liberty!

God wants you to live in freedom—not bound by sin! "If the Son therefore shall make you free, ye shall be free indeed" (John 8:36). "But God be thanked, that ye were the servants of sin, but ye have obeyed from the heart that form of doctrine which was delivered you. Being then made free from sin, ye became the servants of righteousness" (Romans 6:17-18).

> **"A clean heart is a free heart."**
> ~ Mother Teresa

If it was impossible for people to change, there would be no possibility of redemption. God is in the restoration, redeeming business. You can experience the joy of a restored, pure heart. Of course you

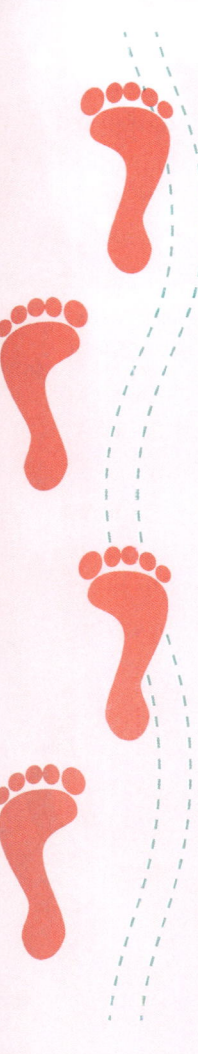

can't go back and make things as if they never happened. There may be consequences involved, but your spirit can be restored and your mind can be renewed.

> "I can't store up good feelings and behavior—but only draw them fresh from God each day."
> ~ Corrie ten Boom

STEPS

1. **Feel godly sorrow.** Mary Magdalene was a sinner when she wept at Jesus' feet (Luke 7:38). Let the tears come. Tears heal and cleanse.
2. **Return to the "light."** In I John 1:5-7, the apostle writes that God is light, and when His children live in the light, the blood of Jesus cleanses from all sin. There is a spiritual washing that cleanses the soul. "Come now, and let us reason together, saith the LORD: though your sins be as scarlet, they shall be as white as snow; though they be red like crimson, they shall be as wool" (Isaiah 1:18).
3. **Have faith.** Our hearts are purified by faith (Acts 15:9). Faith will help you in the days to come. It's faith that can

move mountains, even high elevations of carnal desire. Don't ever think you don't have faith. "Think soberly, according as God hath dealt to every man the measure of faith" (Romans 12:3).

4. **Get the power.** Acts 1:8 tells us, "Ye shall receive power, after that the Holy Ghost is come upon you." Every Spirit-filled believer has access to the power of the God. God's Spirit is compared to fire that refines and purifies, wind that blows dirt and debris out of the way, and water that cleanses.

Once people repent of sin and are covered by the blood of Jesus Christ by baptism in His name, they must act according to Scripture by leaving their life of sin. Repentance brings forgiveness. It doesn't mean you are perfect now, but that God sees you as innocent. There are still things to learn and responsibilities to live up to, but God no longer sees your sin. His focus is on His church that is made righteous by His mercy and grace. You can trust God to accomplish His desire in you, confident that He is at work.

God is not just love. He's a God of lovingkindness. Look at these words from Jeremiah: "The Lord hath appeared of old unto me, saying, Yea, I have loved thee with an everlasting love: therefore with lovingkindness have I drawn thee" (Jeremiah 31:3).

Just as the Lord drew the prophet with His lovingkindness, He will draw those who have slipped today, knowing "if we confess our sins, he is faithful and just to forgive us our sins, and to cleanse us from all unrighteousness" (I John 1:9).

God is not just love.

God's mercy is bigger than any mistake you or I could ever make. He is our heart healer, our soul healer, and our body healer. We may carry scars from our experiences, but God can take away the pain and guilt of our sin. Glory, glory, hallelujah!

"The LORD is longsuffering, and of great mercy, forgiving iniquity and transgression" (Numbers 14:18).

"Thou art a God ready to pardon, gracious and merciful, slow to anger, and of great kindness" (Nehemiah 9:17).

"The God of all grace, who hath called us unto his eternal glory by Christ Jesus, after that ye have suffered a while, make you perfect, stablish, strengthen, settle you" (I Peter 5:10).

If you're feeling sorry about some things you've done wrong, that's good! There should be sorrow when we are doing things that separate us from God. The Lord uses godly sorrow to work repentance in our lives so that we can be saved (II Corinthians 7:10). Let godly sorrow lead you to get things right with God.

God still makes beauty out of ashes.

STOPPING

After repentance, stopping is the first important step on the pure path. God's Word makes us clean (John 15:3), but now we have to stop the things that would suck us back into sin. You have to choose to put in place some of the things we talked about in dealing with temptation and making plans in advance. Stopping something that has become a habit isn't easy. Believe me, it's easier not to start something in the first place. But with God's help and your commitment and discipline, you can do it! Just make sure when you stop a habit or behavior you fill that "space" with healthy, wholesome, encouraging thoughts and activities.

Human beings come wired with a desire to connect with others. It's natural. As a Christian girl, the most important connection you can make is with the Lord. He can take you to a place of confidence and closeness with Him that will cleanse your heart and keep your feet on the pure path. It's not always easy, but it is possible. Besides having the best guide possible in Jesus, He can bring godly people into your life to help you in your effort to live for Him. Consider this: Following the path of sin and ignoring the mercy of God is not an easy road. The best thing to do is let God lead. He knows the way!

SECRETS

If you've done something all wrong but you admit it and turn to God, He can help you turn things to all right!

Satan would love to blackmail you with the sins of your past. If you want to be free of them, confess them to the Lord as to a trusted friend. Time doesn't heal all wounds and burying things inside doesn't make the pain go away. Be free from the burden of carrying your secret sin around and move into freedom and healing. "As far as the east is from the west, so far hath he removed our transgressions from us" (Psalm 103:12).

SEEING

It's important now to see things from a new perspective. You can't go back and undo what's been done, but if you've been forgiven, you're forgiven! It's off the record! Now it's time to move into the future stronger and wiser than before. The saying goes that experience is the best teacher, but let me say, experience can be a brutal teacher. On the other side of that coin, you are forever changed. You see things differently. You know the realities and how easy it is to fall. Oliver Wendell Holmes said, "A mind that is stretched by a new experience can never go back to its old dimensions." It's true. You are changed, now use that change to do things better and perhaps even help someone else who might be having the same struggles.

Your recommitment to Christ will be tested, but now you know the truth about purity's rewards. If you've been burned, you also know that sin doesn't have the power to satisfy your heart's desire for true relationship.

On the subject of "seeing," God knows you have memories (and they can make you feel worse than anything). They will try to haunt you, but don't let them. Replace them with good thoughts and praise to God.

Learning to really walk with the Lord if you have been away from Him in your heart for some time (even if you never left church) can be challenging. God is a gentleman. He won't hurt you or use you, but He will help you work through problems one layer at a time. The key is knowing you don't have to do things in your own strength. You can rely on His strength. You can be strong in spirit when you are in God's strong hands.

Remember, you have to guard your own heart!

SET FREE!

When you are tempted to fill your mind with horrible thoughts of horrible you, instead fill your mind with Jesus. He's the One who can break every chain, break every chain, break every chain! Talking bad about yourself to yourself isn't going to do any good. If you've repented, move forward. A mentality of despair can only be changed by the precious gift of God's miraculous grace.

You are a new creature in Christ! Things may change from here. You may find yourself dressing differently, talking differently, and acting differently. That's good! That's healthy! I just want to make sure you know that you are set free from the sins of your past.

Remember this powerful verse: "There is therefore now no condemnation to them which are in Christ Jesus, who walk not after the flesh, but after the Spirit" (Romans 8:1). When we continue to walk in victory over the desires of our flesh, over time what God intended to form in our character will be there—a pure heart!

It can be hard to let go of guilt. It's a good thing God knows even that about us and has given us a good word to encourage us on the subject: "For if our heart condemn us, God is greater than our heart, and knoweth all things" but "if our heart condemn us not then we have confidence toward God" (I John 3:20-21). God can give you a clean conscience, a clean heart. Have confidence in His Word.

If your desire is to get near to God, He will respond and come near to you (James 4:8). Your desire is a spiritual magnet that draws His heart to yours.

A PERSONAL NOTE TO THOSE WHO HAVE BEEN ABUSED

It saddens me that so many precious girls have been wounded by selfish people—and that so many times they suffer in silence. I know it's not easy to talk about, but, my sweet sister, burying it does not help anyone.

To those untouched by abuse, it may seem unreal, but if you walked into a room and there were three girls with you in that room, statistics tell us it's likely one of the girls has been molested in some way.

I have a testimony. I was molested by two men (at different times) who were supposed to be guardian protectors. How devastating to a girl when a father figure does such a thing to her. It doesn't just mess with her body, it messes with her mind and with all of her.

Please, if you have been abused in any way, don't cover it up. You aren't covering for yourself—you are innocent! What some wicked person did to you was not your fault and had nothing to do with you. It was all about them.

I have a word from the Lord for you. God does not want you to live under the weight of someone else's sin. He wants you to be free. He wants to heal you. He wants to break off misplaced shame and feelings of being dirty. He wants to prepare you for a pure relationship with a godly man who will honor you and cherish you.

God wants you to know you are not guilty of sexual sin when you did not choose to have sex. What happened in the past is done, and there's no changing it. What we have now are new choices to make. Choices to release the anguish. Choices to move into healing. Choices to live purely as much as is under your control.

But it starts with telling someone. A mom is usually a good person to turn to, but if that's not a safe place because of your situation, find a trusted leader or family friend. You may feel it would be easier to tell a peer, but honestly, most friends aren't equipped to help you through something of this magnitude.

There are times a girl may feel she shouldn't say anything because what happened was between her and her boyfriend. At first she liked the kiss, the touch, but then things got out of control. She tried to stop it, but he pressed through her objections and took what she didn't want to give. Sometimes that can be the end of a relationship, and sometimes the girl still cares for the boy and covers for him.

This is where I want to put my "Momma" hat on and say, "That's why it's so important that you don't let yourself get into those types of situations." That may be true, but the point is to let you know that when someone takes something from you sexually, you are not guilty of sexual sin. You may feel impure, violated, or used, and that is understandable; but don't allow self-condemnation to grow in your heart because of what someone else did to you.

I wonder how many people who have suffered sexual abuse now struggle with all kinds of poor coping tools—such as addictions to substances, eating disorders, cutting, or promiscuity. My friend, these "tools" don't work. They might give a temporary relief, but they will never solve any problem; in fact, they usually make bigger problems.

Until the Lord comes for His church, there will always be wicked and selfish people in our world. We can't change what others do in their thoughts, words, or actions, but we can make a commitment to change ourselves. I am a victor, not a victim. I am an overcomer, not a downtrodden girl overcome by what someone else did to me.

I am free. I am whole. I am happy. The only way I know to make that happen is to receive that freedom from the Lord for yourself. Letting go of past hurts is a part of life. Everyone has to do it. Sometimes it's harder than others because sexual wounding goes deep into a person's soul. I want you to get something here that might not be as easy to see in other discussions. Sexual activity touches the very core of who we are—our souls. Willing participants or not, intimate contact goes far beyond just a physical hook-up.

Parting Words

God graciously offers His purity, holiness, and righteousness (II Corinthians 2:5). What precious gifts! God made Himself to be sin so that we could be made righteous. How we handle His gifts is up to us. Will we honor Him and His Word or do our own thing? I pray God gives us thankful hearts that treasure the invaluable, eternal gifts He has made available to us.

When we walk the pure path, it's not a trial but a life of joy that brings blessing and gives God glory. Tomorrow's blessing could well depend on today's consecration.

Pledge

Because of God's love for me, I choose to love Him with all my heart, soul, mind, and strength. To honor God, my family, and my future spouse, I voluntarily sign my name as my commitment to a life of purity in both public and private.

I pledge to abstain from sexual activity until the day I marry. Knowing this is the best choice for spiritual, physical, and emotional health, I vow to keep my body and thoughts pure as I trust in and seek God's will for my life.

_____
Name

_____
Date

CONCLUSION

People are starving for the truth. We live in a world of people who may look hard and crude, but inside what are they longing for? From the kids raised in church to those morally broken, it's time for real sex education and revolution.

What is a revolution? It's a sudden radical and pervasive change. It's a revolving or turning back to a starting point—and that starting point was established by God's Word, not a godless society.

It is my prayer that you will experience all the joys God has prepared for you. I pray the Lord helps you remember your commitment to purity. May you make wise decisions and be true to your pledge and to Jesus.

You have a wide open horizon before you. Set high expectations for yourself. Develop your gifts. Get a good education. Serve somewhere in your church, community, and world. God made you unique, so make choices based on what's best for your future.

Find something that is bigger than you and plug into it. Being a young, single person isn't about wandering aimlessly until Prince Charming gallops into your life and whisks you away to your happily ever after.

Your life has purpose and you have a destiny and calling in God. You are a person of value, that's why it's so important you are careful with the choices you make. You have incredible opportunities in your walk with God. It's a time to grow and serve, when you aren't "bogged down" in any worldly relationship that could monopolize your time or distract you from the pure path.

Recognize your worth! If we look to Proverbs 31 at what some might say is "God's Ideal Woman," notice the things that are important from a biblical perspective. She was skilled, smart, and capable—a leader and a businesswoman. She was prepared for whatever came her way. She didn't live in fear because she made plans in advance to succeed. She was balanced and successful, not just in her home but in public, too.

God doesn't want you to be content with just your salvation. There's so much more He desires to give you and accomplish through you. The rewards in this life and in eternity far outweigh any suffering you will experience by taking the pure path with Him.

"Let us hear the conclusion of the whole matter: Fear God, and keep his commandments: for this is the whole duty of man" (Ecclesiastes 12:13).

TESTIMONY

Going from a private school of about 200 kids to finding ourselves in a public high school with over 4,500 students was a drastic change. We were in the heart of Miami, and fights, cops, and drug dealings were part of everyday life. It was there we learned to not only stand up for our beliefs but to embrace them.

When we were old enough to date, we thought that since our peers had boyfriends, it was the thing to do. We were mistaken. A relationship caused one of us to backslide. Outwardly, you couldn't tell. She still went to church and looked the same, but became cold and lost the love of the Lord she once had.

She wanted to leave church and get a taste of the real world. The problem was, all her friends were in church so she didn't have anyone to go with. Looking back, that may have been God's way of protecting her. It took time, but thanks to the prayers of our parents, she found her way back to the altar.

One day, our parents informed us we were going to move. We loved the life we had been blessed to live in Miami and did not want to give it up. It was one of the hardest things we ever have had to do. We packed and started out for Michigan. One day we were wearing flip-flops, and the next we found ourselves learning to walk in snow boots.

Our new home was nothing like Miami. Every detail of our lives had changed. If it had not been for the local Apostolic church, we don't know how we would have gotten through the trial. We felt like Job who had had everything taken from him. But just as with Job, the Lord has given us everything back, and has more than doubled His blessings upon us. Through it all, we have learned it pays to stand strong and serve the Lord with all of your heart. Falling in love with Jesus is the best thing we have ever done.

~ Stephanie and Melanie Well
Stephanie serves as music director and Melanie serves as pianist at First Apostolic Church of Mt. Morris, Michigan.

Endnotes

1. *http://www.merriam-webster.com/dictionary/pure*
2. Steve Gallagher. *How America Lost Her Innocence: A History of the Sexual Revolution* (Pure Life Ministries, 2005), 17.
3. Nicholas Confessore. *Porn and Politics in a Digital Age, www.pbs.org*
4. Common English Bible (Nashville, TN: Christian Resources Development Corporation, 2010).
5. *http://www.blueletterbible.org/lang/lexicon/lexicon.cfm?Strong's=G2588&t=KJV*
6. Ibid.
7. *http://www.jewishencyclopedia.com/articles/7436-heart*
8. John K. Ryan, trans. *The Confessions of St. Augustine* (New York: Image, Doubleday, 1960), 43.
9. *http://usatoday30.usatoday.com/life/television/news/2005-11-09-sex-on-tv_x.htm*, Ann Oldenburg, *USA TODAY*.
10. *http://www.cityvision.edu/wiki/truth-behind-fantasy-porn*
11. *http://www.blueletterbible.org/lang/lexicon/lexicon.cfm?Strong's=G2479&t=KJV*
12. Lauren F. Winner. *Real Sex: The Naked Truth about Chastity* (Paperback) (Grand Rapids, MI: Brazos Press, 2005), 87.
13. Elisabeth Elliott. *Passion and Purity* (Grand Rapids, MI: Baker Books, 1984).
14. *http://people.howstuffworks.com/kissing.htm*
15. *http://people.howstuffworks.com/kissing4.htm*
16. Lori Wagner. *Gates and Fences: Straight Talk in a Crooked World* (Affirming Faith), 46.
17. *http://www.focusonthefamily.com/lifechallenges/love_and_sex/purity/what_your_teens_need_to_know_about_sex.aspx#footnote1*
18. *http://www.cdc.gov/reproductivehealth/unintendedpregnancy/contraception.htm#44*
19. *http://www.cdc.gov/std/stats/STI-Estimates-Fact-Sheet-Feb-2013.pdf*
20. Ibid.
21. Ryan. *The Confessions of St. Augustine*, 43.

The Girl in the Dress: Uncovering the Mystery of Modesty

In an easy-to-read style, practical insights and scriptural references explore biblical modesty. As we live and dress according to the Word of God, our inner beauty will take over, and the outward result will be one that makes us truly beautiful. For all ages.

Covered by Love: The Uncut Mystery – It's So Much More Than Hair

In a clear, thorough manner, this book lays out the positive message of obedience, purpose, and blessing concerning women's hair. Read it with your boys so they will gain an appreciation for the godly women who embrace these principles. For all ages.

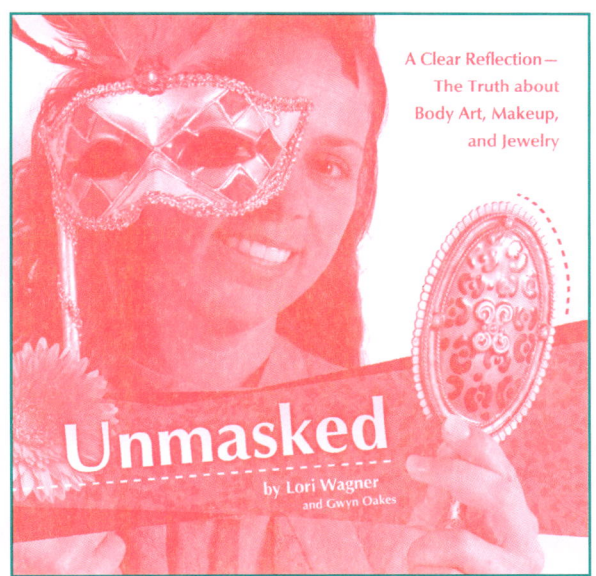

Unmasked: A Clear Reflection – The Truth about Body Art, Makeup, and Jewelry

Drawing from spiritual insight and historical facts, this book offers information about the "masking" of our society. It offers an open door to model biblical truth for a spiritually hungry generation who wants to live a holy, godly life. For all ages.

These books are available through Ladies Ministries.
Call 636-229-7895 or email *ladies@upci.org*.
Quantity discount prices also available.

To be assured of Bible-based literature,
always look for these registered trademarks.